THE MARRIAGE MAZE

McLaird's Field Guide For The Journey

D1375645

George McLaird, M.Div.

Malcomb Morrow Publishing House
Mill Valley, California

The Marriage Maze
Copyright © 1995 by George McLaird, M.Div.

All rights reserved. No portion of this manual may be reproduced by any means whatsoever without written, prior permission from the publisher. For information and to order additional copies, contact:

Malcomb Morrow Publishing House
P.O. Box 2536
Mill Valley, California 94942-2536

World Wide Web Home Page Number:
http://www.well.com/user/gm/

Library of Congress Card No. 95-79114

ISBN: 1-887182-01-2

Grateful acknowledgement is made for permission to reproduce a section from the following material:
The Pelican Brief, by John Grisham, Bantam Doubleday Dell Publishing Group, Inc., copyright 1992.

Cover and Book Design by Patricia J. Oji
Book Production by Cypress House, Fort Bragg, California 95437
Manufactured in the U.S.A.
First Edition
9 8 7 6 5 4 3 2 1

Dedication

PHOTO BY VERA PHOTOGRAPHY

Linda and George McLaird

To Linda,
my closest friend and loving wife.

I've seen you in the spring and summer
fall and autumn too
a cut above
a shade more rich
deep loveliness in you.

Planted on the other side
now watered by the dew
like a tree intact, in place
is this love in me for you.

–George

Acknowledgements

I wish to thank God for life; my mother, Florence, for teaching me to..."Always leave a place in better condition than you found it." For my wife, Linda, who supports me in dozens of practical ways — an elegant partner and elaborate gift too great to explain or acknowledge enough; for friends of every stripe; such as the members, staff, and participants of the Sausalito Presbyterian Church for supporting me and allowing me so much freedom, and for considering this work theirs, not just mine; my son, Sean, who continues to stretch my mind and loosen me up a bit; the founding fathers of *The Alliance for Educational Development* — Jim Osborn, the "charging guard" who keeps all the pieces from dissolving; Jon Schulberg, for creativity and insights extraordinaire; The General — Rev. Wayne Hoffmann for invaluable help on content, guidance with the military, and inspiration and general marketing and networking; their wives, Nancy Osborn, Nancy Hoffmann and Caryn Schulberg for their support and valuable suggestions; our CEO, Jill Fugaro, and business consultant, Dan Sheridan; Ted Cochran and James R. Murrin for their creative inspiration; the folks at KTVU, especially Kevin O'Brien; Judi Heaphy; Deborah Perez, Chaplain (COL) John W. Schumacher, Chaplain (COL) John Wells, Chaplain (LTC) William DeLeo, Doris Donaldson and Jack Carter for editing; Lynne Parode for presentation and content corrections and overall excellent advice; suggestions from hundreds of seminar participants on improving the content of this workbook; Nicholas Cann, Robin Sinclair and Pam Will for logos and art work; Bob Haydock — animated computer graphics; Scott Taylor of *Resolution* for hundreds of hours of computer work; Suzanne Vargo — clergy computer consultant; editorial comments, Thomas A. Rohrer; the advisory board of AED — Kare Anderson, Mary Ann Barr, Ph.D., Bruce Burtch, Carolyn Conger, Christy Dames, Judi Flowers, Kimberly Kassner, Leigh Markell, Sharon Menary, Sarah Nolan, Patricia J. Oji, Caryn Schulberg, Jerry Seltzer, Arundahti Simmons, Kay Cash Smith, Richard Smith, M.D., Susan Sims Smith, LCSW, Sonnee Weedn, Ph.D.; Dr. Barry Kaufman, Dominican College; Lisa Schwartz, Principal of the Marin County Community School.

THE MARRIAGE MAZE
Field Guide

Page

THE MARRIAGE MAZE
Field Guide

THE MARRIAGE MAZE
Field Guide

THE MARRIAGE MAZE
Field Guide

Introduction

Meyer Friedman, M.D.*

EXPRESSED IN THE SIMPLEST OF WORDS AND PHRASES, Rev. George McLaird's multiple messages delivered in his book abound in wisdom. He recognizes the difficulties in adopting many of his "Fifty Practices" and describes drills and introspective checklists that will make adoption of many of the "Practices" easier to accomplish.

I was particularly impressed by those "Practices" that aim at:

(1) improving listening skills;
(2) giving thoughtful gifts at unexpected times;
(3) writing one's obituary; and, especially,
(4) "dating" one's spouse long after the marriage has begun.

The author has written a guide book whose primary purpose is to prevent the deterioration of a marriage. Such deterioration ruined his first marriage and the "Fifty Practices" he describes in this book has preserved his second marriage. No student of the human situation would deny that, if the "Practices" elucidated in this book were adopted by the spouses of a marriage, their marriage would retain its fragrance and spiritual loveliness even beyond the demise of one of the spouses.

Indeed, this truly resplendent book contains the sort of pragmatic wisdom that old Benjamin Franklin would have appreciated. Certainly, there isn't a hint of jargon throughout the book. It has been compiled by a very wise man who has read many fine books and has counseled hundreds of couples who had let their partnership weaken. I recommend without reservation the book's reading by every spouse.

---

* Dr. Friedman coined the terms "Type A and Type B Behavior." He is the author of several books, among them *Type A Behavior and Your Heart* (Knopf, 1974).

Foreword

Hal Stone, Ph.D. and Sidra Stone, Ph.D.*

I T SEEMS FAIR TO SAY that the past 30 to 40 years have witnessed a revolution in the realm of personal relationship. As we moved into the psycho-spiritual revolution that began in the sixties and seventies, an ever-increasing number of people began to search for something more than a strict form in their relationships. It was no longer enough to have children and raise them. Monogamy itself became a threatened mode of behavior as ever greater numbers of people began to enter into some form of consciousness work and experimentation with new kinds of relationships.

Increasing numbers of people began to recognize when they didn't experience love in their lives, and that it was no longer acceptable to go on in loveless relationships. Under these circumstances, men and woman sought other relationships, relationships where they could find some deeper meaning, a more fulfilling sexuality, a sense of communion, a feeling of common ground and destiny. Numerous couples have gone through painful, heart-wrenching experiences, many of which ended in separation, and many of which ended in new and very different kinds of relationships.

One of the reasons that so many marriages blew apart was that the next stage of the marriage revolution had not yet come into place. How does one work on a relationship? If we lose our love, what do we do about it? How can we make relationships work? What is it that kills love when it was once present? It took many years before consciousness teachers began to address these issues and we are fortunate today to have a body of literature and experience that addresses these questions.

What has emerged out of this cauldron of passion and pain, separation and loss, and love and commitment is a new

---

* Authors of *Embracing Heaven & Earth, Embracing Ourselves,* as well as the developers of Voice Dialogue.

vision of what relationship is all about. This new vision has at its core three fundamental ideas:

1. All of our relationships are teachers if we know how to relate to them properly, if we know how to use them properly. Seen in this light, whatever happens to us in our relationships, no matter how dark matters may seem at any point, there is teaching that is available to us out of the experience.

2. Whom we choose in relationship is not an accident, but rather a meaningful event. Our relationships are designed to fill out the missing elements of our personality, the parts of ourselves that are unconscious to us. The significant relationships of our hues, seen in this light, become mirrors, reflecting ponds to help us re-discover these elements of our personality that have gone into hiding for a wide range of reasons.

3. Relationship itself is a path, a proper path to consciousness. The path of relationship does not have to rule out our treading on other paths. However, it does mean that we must learn to surrender ourselves to the process of relationship. This surrender is not to another person, but rather to a process of learning that only relationship can bring to us.

Now these considerations are important because they bring honor and meaning to the world of relationship. In order to use these ideas, however, we need to know how to be with people in new and different ways. As George very clearly points out, it requires real work to develop and to maintain healthy relationships.

As we will know, however, it is one thing to talk about using relationship as a teacher and another thing to figure out how we do it. What do I do when I get angry and want to yell at my partner? Why is listening so difficult? Why are women/men so different? Why has the passion disappeared from our relationship?

Enter George McLaird's new book, *The Marriage Maze*. In a sense, it is a misnomer to call this a book in the usual sense. It is, rather, an eminently practical

Manual/Workbook/Wisdom Reference book that moves through a remarkable group of relationship practices, each one of which has a theoretical core and an experiential component that any individual or couple can read and work through in a simple, yet remarkably productive fashion.

Listen to the following quote from Section 3 of the book that deals with worksheets, tools, charts, backgrounds and explanations:

> "Some of the streets in our nation are perilous, especially at night. However, for many people, there is a place far more dangerous than any street they may walk: the most treacherous location on earth for them is behind the closed doors of their own home."

We were struck by the power of this statement. It is so obvious. Why had we never seen it in this light before? This is George's gift. He catches a deeper truth and then puts it into a form that seems ingenuously simple. This book could well have been titled, *"A Guide for the Perplexed,"* if Maimonides hadn't beaten him to it. It is a guide for meandering through the maze of relationship. It provides an opportunity to stop at different places and read the maps he has provided that pinpoint some of the real danger points we meet as we traverse this maze. He allows us to get our bearings by committing ourselves to certain relationship practices that make maze-running a much more understandable, much less perplexing, and certainly a much more pleasant experience.

This is a wonderfully practical book that serves the needs of all of us who search for healthier relationships. It is a book that will also speak to the health-care practitioner who is concerned with issues of relationship and who require a structure for dealing with the wide range of ideas and methods and options that confront anyone trying to help people deal with their relationships.

We have been involved in our own personal relationship work from the moment we met many years ago. Yet we found this book to be refreshingly simple, deeply insightful, fun to read, and personally helpful. What more can we say?

Prologue

WE HUMANS ARE SO COMPLEX — and are becoming more so with each passing day — that no single approach to relationships can contain all that needs to be said. My approach is but one of many. My hope is that it will be useful to you.

What it's about.

Even though I am extremely concerned about the world-wide deterioration of relationships, my approach is not about preserving marriages, families, and households at all costs.

Therefore, this book is not about:

- artificially prolonging terminally ill relationships that should be allowed to die with dignity and grace;
- extending relationships with guilt or sleight-of-hand manipulations that are near death;
- quick-fix tricks marketed with outlandish claims.

Therefore, this book is about:

- preventing relationship diseases in the first place;
- developing and maintaining strong, healthy marital relationships;
- providing foundational structures for every type of relationship;
- healing those relationships that are curable;
- assisting those who have correctly realized that a particular relationship is beyond their present ability to cure, and to choose to move toward relationship-euthanasia in the most caring way possible.

More than a quarter of a century ago my marriage of more than a decade had deteriorated into a series of nasty verbal skirmishes. It had, of course, not begun like that. Actually, we had a few years of bliss and several years of good times.

What I'm about.

Looking back, I see what happened. The good years we shared were not because we were compatible and thoughtful, nor because we bent over backward to accommodate ourselves to one another's life path. Those years were good because our attention was focused on education, work, buying a home, and the birth of our son. A year or so following his birth, we started focusing on our relationship. That's when the war began.

Through it all, we desperately wanted to learn to live happily ever after. We sought advice in magazines and books, from friends and professional counselors, without making a dent in the way we related to each other.

During the last four years of our marriage, things were so bad that all I wanted was to get out. With genuine despair, we both realized that all we'd ever had were the ingredients of a short-lived relationship. At first, it seemed like a lot; certainly enough for a lifetime. We had mutual regard for one another, a handful of commonly held goals, behavioral engineering techniques, the obligation of honoring our vows, strong religious connections, family ties and traditions.

What we lacked, but didn't know at the time, were the ingredients for sustaining a life-long marriage. In part, those ingredients are authentic compatibility, self-awareness and its twin companion, *psychological health*, a commitment to truthfulness, flexibility, and life-practices that renew commitment.

Buyer Beware   Symbolically speaking, our marriage was the equivalent of a beautiful house we'd bought believing it to have a strong foundation. Instead, the foundation turned out to have been made of soft wood that held up fine on sunny days, but was too weak to withstand stress.

In marriage, inner and outer conditions go hand in glove. Our environment, education, community, and beliefs play major roles in our lives, but the memories, emotions, and attitudes underlying our decisions and actions are more difficult to map. The importance of our psychological foundation cannot be over emphasized. When our foundation is weak, we are easily overwhelmed by outer conditions.

When our subterranean structure is unstable, based on childhood memories, spiritual anorexia, early loss or deprivation, submerged incidents that trigger within us violence or rage, it cannot be counted on to support a healthy household.

On the other hand, when our psychological foundation is strong and *Skills Are Not Enough* stable, based on wholesome memories, or fully explored and rebuilt with the help of skilled practitioners and continually strengthened with consistent spiritual nourishment, it can be counted on to uphold a healthy household.

Our behavior modification techniques were much more than quick fixes, but we failed to do the work that must be done in tandem with these techniques. We neglected the deep psychological probing and failed to clean out the dreadful memories that made us defensive and self-centered and, in some cases, lead to addictions and excesses.

We practiced communication skills without effect. We tried to compromise, which more often than not led to great frustration. We never learned authentic accommodation, genuine tolerance, or how to balance two sets of desires and needs.

In hopeless frustration, carrying feelings of failure, we agreed to end our marriage.

After being single for seven years, I married a second time. That was thirteen years ago. With a few bad days thrown in now and then, these years have been the easiest, the happiest, and the most productive of my life.

What happened? What made the difference? How could such a turn-around take place?

This book details how to move from short-term affection to life-long married love, and these steps can also be applied to understanding and improving any relationship. Most of what I've learned has come from experience, from observing myself and counseling others, supplemented by reading, listening, and talking with other professionals in this field.

This book is also about renewing and improving the most important relationship we have— the one on which all our relationships depend— our relationship with ourselves. By continuously inspecting and repairing our foundations — an area essentially ignored or inadequately dealt with by many books in this field — we can avoid the loneliness and neediness that may impel us into relationships not in our best interest. Here, we're dealing with guts, not glitter.

If my first wife and I had been able to read this book and practice the exercises it contains, and had we been able to face our own individual, internal unfinished business, we might never have divorced. But that was not our fate.

Seven years after my divorce, when it became clear that Linda and I were going to marry, I knew I had to face the explosives I had used to undermine my first marriage. Experience and reading had taught me that I would certainly repeat my previous mistakes unless I was willing to examine the role I'd played in the failure of my first marriage. I knew that if I left them covered, I would repeat my mistakes in such subtle ways that I could blame my new

Hypnotherapy Is A Tool   wife if my second marriage failed.

I began by seeking the help of a hypnotherapist. With his guidance, I discovered many of the deep roots of my previously unconscious destructive actions. Since then I have participated in many internal investigations, and I have listened to the complaints and fantasies of hundreds of men and women who had lost their lovers or their ability to love. In many of their stories, I heard echoes of my own.

I know myself better now than ever before, and

I know what it takes to have a happy, healthy relationship.

Why do my wife and I get along so well, and why is our marriage (with the exception, as I've already mentioned, of a few bad days now and then) so easy? In addition to what I've already mentioned has been our willingness to explore our role in the deterioration of our former relationships. We continue on the pathway of self-discovery, knowing that self-examination will last a life-time. *Spirituality Is A Must*

Additionally, we continually renew our spiritual foundations. I am an ordained Presbyterian pastor, yet I do not consider myself very religious in a modern sense. Many contemporary religionists barricade themselves in their religions, adopting unreasonably harsh rules and engaging more in exclusivity and intolerance than love.

I believe that spirituality is a way of getting in touch and having an experience with Spirit that resembles the experience of the religion's founder. That is, we trace and mirror their experience for ourselves until we are ready to move on to our own unique path.

Spirituality provides hope, encouragement, and a sense of confident presence. It is a path that intends to leave every person, place, and thing we encounter in a little better condition than we found it. Finally, spirituality entails private nourishing in order to fuel-up for the work of daily living and collective healing. Everything I've written here will prove fruitless without the spiritual component. This book is a vehicle that will enable you to communicate well and enjoy healthy relationships, but you must fill the vehicle with your own fuel. *Running On Empty*

A word of caution: This book will not enable you to live conflict-free, every day, forever; it is not piein-the-sky nonsense. Instead, you'll learn how to deal with conflict, and how to follow your own path toward wholeness. The vehicle is safe, but it's not automatic.

If you're looking for a free ride, if you think your relationship is moving along just fine, answer the following questions:

- Is your relationship thriving or just surviving?
- Has the quality of your relationship deteriorated since you got married?
- Do you find that many of your discussions escalate into arguing?
- Has your relationship with your partner changed drastically since your child(ren) was born?
- Does your sex life seem like a boring movie?
- Are you retaining any secrets from your partner about important issues?

If your relationship passes the test, congratulations! If you or your relationship need a tune up, you've come to the right service station!

Let's pop the hood and look inside.

George McLaird, M.Div.
Mill Valley, CA 1995

Section One

23 EXERCISES TO PRACTICE BY YOURSELF

Chapter 1

EMULATE SUCCESS

A t the beginning of one of my workshops, Bess, an attractive woman in her mid-thirties asked, "Where are these happy, successful couples you talk about? I certainly don't know anyone whose relationship I'd want."

I'd heard the same observation often. Individuals and couples have told me that they do not know a single happily married couple. I understand why they feel that way; for years I said the same thing.

We all know that "birds of a feather flock together," and personal reality colors the picture we have of other relationships. Happily married people tell me that most of the couples they know seem to relate quite well. People in explosive relationships may find people in healthy relationships "boring." Others may look away because happiness makes their unhappiness more vivid.

Most people in solid, enduring relationships spend a fair amount of time with one another, but Jennifer and Christopher were one of those rare couples who spent nearly twenty-four hours a day together. I met them when I was married to my first wife, and to this day they enjoy one another. They owned their own business, and this, rather than possessiveness or insecurity, accounted for their spending so much time together.

The keys to Jennifer and *Not your "ideal" couple.* Christopher's compatibility? First, they were both psychologically healthy. No one is 100 percent physically or psychologically healthy, but Jennifer and Christopher came close. That is, they continually faced their bad habits, compulsive behaviors, and they nourished themselves spiritually, mentally, emotionally and socially.

3

Second, they lived in balance. They played (dated) with the same delight as they worked. Third, they lived in accord. They had somehow divided their chores and did not interfere when the other person was in charge. Fourth, they constantly helped one another without being asked and without interfering. Another thing they did that I once thought "old-fashioned" was that they thanked and complimented each other often. To this day, they remain a couple that I emulate.

Food For Thought

Do you know any happily married couples?

❏ YES   ❏ NO

If so, who are they?

_____

_____

What is there about their relationship that you wish to emulate?

_____

_____

_____

_____

Comments

One of the easiest ways to improve any skill is to emulate those who do it well. Emulating those who are living happily is one of the easiest ways to improve our relationships.

Most people who describe their marriages as "happy" use the same word to describe their parents' marriage. But, for us whose parents were not happily married, we must somehow profit from their mistakes and look elsewhere for guidance.

The suggestions in this Guide are the specific things happily married couples report they do (or don't do).

I Emulate Those Who Have Successful Relationships.   *Affirmation*

For more on this subject see *EMULATE SUCCESS* in   *References*
Section 3, p. 147

Chapter 2

SPEAK GENTLY

At a counseling session with a married couple in my study at the church, Bentley became so enraged that he stood up and called his wife Barbara a slut. Now, Bentley wasn't accusing Barbara of sexual unfaithfulness. Her only crime was that she disagreed with him and refused to be treated as his willful daughter.

"You make me sick, so sick I want to puke on you!" Bentley raged. "I don't ever want to see you again." With that he slammed the door and left.

Dry-eyed, Barbara said, "Now you see what happens. This happens all the time."

"Do you know that you have just been verbally and emotionally battered?" I asked.

"Yes," Barbara said, "but I don't know what to do about it. Now that he has done this in front of you, I think the marriage is over."

When Speaking With Our Beloved, Even Our "Yeses" and "Noes" Need To Have Dull Edges.

But the marriage wasn't over. Bentley needed Barbara to abuse, and Barbara was willing to take verbal and emotional abuse to "save" the marriage. Verbal abuse is violence, however, and accepting it in order to save a marriage is blind surrender.

I encouraged Barbara to join a women's group, the kind of group where women can safely express their feelings and where Barbara could learn how she participates in the deadly dance. I wondered aloud whether Bentley would be willing to attend a meeting specifically created to help men stop being violent toward women, and Barbara said she'd ask him. Miraculously, he consented. Over the next four months, I didn't hear a word from either of them.

Some of the streets in our nation are perilous, especially at night. However, for many people, there is a place far more dangerous than any street they may walk , the most treacherous location on earth for them is behind the closed doors of their own home.

One day Barbara called to tell me that they were still together and added, "Things have never been better."

"Why is that?" I asked, having had doubts that their marriage could be saved. Barbara told me that what they had learned in their separate groups had made them aware of the patterns they'd adopted. She told me about a loose-leaf manual Bentley had been given, detailing violent behaviors. A few days later she dropped off a copy for me. I read the items listed under physical and emotional violence, and because I had never done any of those things, the reading was interesting but not poignant. But when I came to the section dealing with verbal violence, it hit me between the eyes. At that moment, several years after I had been divorced, I realized for the very first time that I had verbally battered and abused my former wife.

BATTERING CHECKLIST*
*Revised from a chart created by
The Community United Against Violence

Yes No

❏   ❏   Does my partner constantly criticize me, blame me for things that are not my fault or verbally degrade me?

❏   ❏   *Do I constantly criticize my partner, assign them blame for things not their fault or verbally degrade them?*

(continued on page 9)

(continued from page 8)

Yes	No	
❏	❏	Has my partner ever pushed, slapped, kicked, bitten, restrained, thrown objects at, spit at or used a weapon against me because he or she was angry or upset?
❏	❏	*Have I ever pushed, slapped, kicked, bitten, restrained, thrown objects at, spit at or used a weapon against my partner because I was angry or upset?*
❏	❏	Is my partner suspicious and jealous? Does my partner make it difficult for me to see friends and family, irrationally accuse me of having affairs,or monitor my mail and phone calls?
❏	❏	*Am I suspicious and jealous of my partner? Do I make it difficult for my partner to see friends and family, irrationally accuse them of having affairs, or monitor his/her mail and phone calls?*
❏	❏	Does my partner prevent me from getting or maintaining a job, control our shared resources, or restrict my access to money?
❏	❏	*Do I prevent my partner from getting or maintaining a job? Do I control our shared resources or restrict his/her access to money?*

(continued on page 10)

(continued from page 9)

Yes	No	
❏	❏	Has my partner ever forced me to have sex without my consent?
❏	❏	*Have I ever forced my partner to have sex without his/her consent?*
❏	❏	Has my partner ever threatened to harm me, my family, friends, children, pets or property? Has my partner threatened to blackmail or "out" me if I leave?
❏	❏	*Have I ever threatened to harm my partner, their family, friends, children, pets or property? Have I ever threatened to blackmail him/her if they leave me?*
❏	❏	Does my partner have a history of violence against former partners?
❏	❏	*Do I have a history of violence against my former partners?*
❏	❏	Must I seek help in ending violence in my relationship *NOW*?
❏	❏	*Must I seek help in ending violence in my relationship* NOW*?*

What NOT To Do

Here are some things NOT to do: Try to work things out alone. Enter couple's counseling together. (If you are in counseling together and you tell the truth, you're liable to be punished or even attacked again once you are alone.) Think that abusive behavior is normal and goes on in every home. Believe that you alone are always "the one who starts it." Believe that you deserve to be talked to or treated abusively.

Here are some things you CAN do: Speak with the leader of your church, synagogue, or temple. At work, speak with your Employee Assistance Program or Human Resources director. Look in the phone book or Yellow Pages for organizations with names like "Community United Against Violence," "Family Violence Project," and "Men Overcoming Violence." Call the Emergency Room at your local hospital or the administrative office of your local police and ask for a referral to a professional counselor. *What To Do*

Even relationships that begin perfectly can be destroyed. Twenty-five percent of all murders occur within the family; i.e., a family member kills another family member.

If this book were a Guide about becoming physically healthy, I might say that in order to be truly healthy we have to eliminate several things from our diets, such as smoking, excessive consumption of alcohol and other drugs, animal fats, etc. *Comments*

In a similar way, if we want to have healthy relationships we must eliminate the things that either weaken or kill them. One of these is violence. Violence can be verbal, emotional, or physical.

Violence never helps (except during life-threatening emergencies such as protecting children from an attacker).

Violence makes relationships unsafe.

Violence is the Number One killer of relationships in our world.

I am Always Looking For Non-violent Solutions When Facing Conflict. *Affirmation*

For information about how any form of violence kills relationships, see SPEAK GENTLY in *Section 3, p. 148.* *References*

11

Chapter 3

REPAIR YOURSELF

While counseling Jack and Fran, I shared with them how I underwent an intense self-investigation and an examination of my past with the help of a professional hypnotherapist. It's an experience everyone would benefit from, and if you'd like to try it, be sure you choose a licensed, professional hypnotist. For me it was a genuine treat of self-discovery.

"Beware Of The Naked Man Who Wants To Sell You A Shirt."
AFRICAN SAYING

I discovered that my workaholic tendencies stemmed from several things, including being raised on a farm where the animals came first and the humans came second. My family never took vacations. I was brought up in a fundamentalist sect that decreed we must attempt to convert every person on earth because those who died unconverted were in for eternal Hell.

All Work And No Play Is A Sickness

On the day of my father's funeral, when I was just five years of age, a man carrying a hat who apparently was a friend of our family said to me, "George, now that your father is gone, you are the man in the family. You must take care of your mother and sister."

At that moment, at some deep level, I bought his sick suggestion. Essentially, that statement robbed me of my childhood. Today, I'm relearning how to play and live in balance with work.

Genetically and energetically I take after my grandmother. She was physically healthy, which contributed to her being a live-wire with nearly endless energy. She was always on the go, joked a lot, slept little, worked hard, and was curious about everything.

All this has led me to my life-long self-repair project — recovering from being a workaholic and bringing balance to my daily living.

"I guess I need to bring some balance into my life," Jack said after I'd told him my story.

Food For Thought   Are you compulsive about anything? _____

_____

_____

Does one thing or project dominate your life to the exclusion of other important or enjoyable activities?

_____

_____

_____

Where are you willing to begin? _____

_____

_____

Comments   Prior to performing surgery, it is normal procedure for doctors and nurses to "scrub" so they will be as germ-free as possible. Similarly, a necessary step toward creating healthier relationships is internal self-scrubbing. This is necessary because the foundation of a strong relationship is the emotional, mental, and spiritual health of each individual.

Somewhere along the line, usually before they got married, successful partners realized that no person and certainly no partner will be capable of bringing them internal peace, happiness, stability, or whatever else they craved. They do not expect to get everything from or to give everything to one person.

Longing for another human to rescue us from our internal world and strengthen us for ordinary life is fantasyland.

The miracle is not found in another person. It is found when we face our own internal torment and tormentors. It is found when, in the privacy of our thoughts, we place all our cards on the table, face up, and call an ace an ace and a spade a spade and, once and for all, we scrub clean the deep, internal wounds that are still spewing infection.

I Practice Self-Repair.   *Affirmation*

For more about this see *REPAIR YOURSELF* in *Section 3,*   *References*
p. 166.

Chapter 4

TALK RESPECTFULLY

H ealthy relationships stand on two equally important and essential legs. One is self-repair (facing our internal wounds and demons). The other is practicing relationship techniques, with skill.

Self-repair must be addressed first and, for most of us to some degree, it is on-going. If we learn and master relationship techniques first and only, our unaddressed residual fear, anger, frustration, or whatever, will erupt and override any level of relationship skill we have.

If we have not taken the first step by finding and addressing our sadness, our terror, our resentment, those emotions will sabotage our best intentions and undermine our attempt to change our behavior. It well may be that we have been treated unkindly by others, perhaps even by our own parents from whom we should have received unending love. It well may be that the deck of cards life dealt us is stacked against us, but until we repair that damage we will remain unable to receive the love we deserve or give the love we would like to give.

One of these relationship techniques is changing our words, the tone of voice we use, and the way we behave with people we care for.

Kelly and Kyle came to see me for *Harsh Words Are Killers* the pre-marital counseling that I require. Almost immediately, they were at odds with one another, deeply enmeshed in pre-marital warfare.

Instead of speaking respectfully to one another, they interrupted one another and made constant corrections of one another's statements, no matter how trivial the error or misstatement. They constantly picked at one another. Each wanted to answer my questions first. If Kelly started to answer a question, Kyle would either talk louder or immediately afterwards add his two cents. Kelly did the same, competing for my attention, interrupting and not listening.

When I pointed this out they closed ranks and in concert told me of their true love for one another and how passionately sexual they were with one another. This was all the proof they needed to know that they truly cared for one another.

I mentioned that it was common at the beginning of marriage — which psychologically and emotionally begins during engagement if not earlier — for a struggle to take place over territory and dominance of the relationship.

Even as they sharpened and thrust swords at one another, they denied the existence of any hostility. I pointed out what I observed and encouraged them to settle their war by negotiating territory and dominance before the wedding day.

Some people never get around to doing this. They live year after year in a constant contest of push and pull over dominance and submission issues.

I've lost track of Kelly and Kyle, but I'll never forget an incident that took place immediately following the wedding ceremony. As the three of us were having our photo taken, Kelly and Kyle started arguing quietly about some detail about the reception. Anyone looking at that wedding photo might think they were smiling at one another and wonder at the alarm on my face, but in truth they were snarling at one another, not smiling.

Food For Thought   Do you talk respectfully to your partner? _____

Are you still vying for dominance in your relationship? _____

Have you engaged on a voyage of self-discovery?

_____

The way we talk with one another is so important that it cannot be overemphasized.

Relationships can be compared more to apples than oranges. Oranges have tough skins and can survive rough treatment. Apples have thin, delicate skins and must be treated carefully.

A huge mistake is to assume that we can talk trash to our partner and treat others harshly, and that doing so will cause no harm.

Respect, like many things in healthy relationships, doesn't just happen. It happens because people care for one another so much that they make a conscious effort to be on their best behavior — and they are, nearly all the time.

Talking disrespectfully may be nothing more serious than a bad habit that must be replaced with a good habit. Hopefully, in your case, this is so. If, however, it is more serious than that, you're in for some hard and vital work.

Comments

I Make a Conscious Effort To Talk Respectfully With My Partner.

Affirmation

For more on this subject, see *TALK RESPECTFULLY*, Section 3, p. 171.

References

19

Chapter 5

MASTER CONFLICT CONTROL

C onflict usually triggers the knee-jerk reactions of fight or flight. Often our responses are based on what we've seen our parents do. I once counseled a woman who barely spoke. Actually, Jane was spontaneous and immediate when talking about the time of day or the weather, but as soon as I asked her anything about herself, it would take her two or three minutes to respond.

When I asked her about this she said that her father, Joel, would hit her if she answered a question in a manner that was not to his liking. He treated her mother the same way.

The conflict-management strategy that Jane learned from her mother was to make no waves. She was conditioned to cause no conflict anywhere, at anytime. When conflict did erupt, Jane and her mother would "play possum" as long as they could. They went inside and waited, alone in their minds, hoping that Father would not take offense.

"What are you doing, mentally, while sitting so silently," I asked.

"Rehearsing answers," Jane said, "and trying to come up with the answer that could not possibly provoke you."

Jane had come to see me because, even though her husband had never struck her nor given any indication that he was contemplating striking her, she still did not trust him or her answers. He had complained about her long silences so often, she thought it time to face the issue.

I assured her that it was not possible for her to say anything to me that would cause me to hit her. As the weeks went by, her response-time became shorter and shorter with both her husband and me.

I never met her father for he had passed away by the time I met Jane, but she assured me that I understood his method of conflict-management, which was to intimidate her into silent submission.

He was so emotionally injured himself that as long as the surface of his relationships were pleasant or silent, he could disregard all that was beneath. But within his household, his wife and daughter lived in constant terror that he would explode.

If you find yourself identifying with Jane or her father, your methods of controlling or protecting yourself are just as unhealthy as theirs. Examine your conflict-management style. If your approach does not bring healthy and satisfying solutions for everyone involved, it's time to switch strategies and learn new techniques.

Food For
Thought

How do you manage conflicts? _____

_____

_____

Comments

Healthy relationships are not conflict-free. Anyone who claims to know how to make a relationship completely conflict-free is selling snake oil. With one another, healthy partners are assertive but not aggressive. Violence and aggressiveness are reserved for emergencies.

Being aggressive carries with it the implication of an unprovoked attack, invasion, or violation of one's boundaries. We are aggressive when we become militant, menacing, or pushy ("in your face"). We are being aggressive when we are so intent on getting our own way that we run over the feelings, opinions, and rights of our partner.

People who are aggressive with their loved ones are actively destroying their relationships.

On the other hand, being assertive carries with it the implication of strong, positive certainty. Assertive folks stand up for their rights, boundaries, and opinions but do so respectfully, with consideration for their partner and themselves. Assertiveness is harmless.

I Practice Skilled Methods Of Conflict-Management.   *Affirmation*

Turn to *MASTER CONFLICT CONTROL, Section 3, p. 172* for more information and some practical suggestions about skilled methods of conflict-management.   *References*

Chapter 6

LISTEN WITH CARE

Jerry came to check me out as a possible candidate for conducting his wedding, a fact I learned only later. During our initial meeting he was very nervous and talked a mile a minute, jumping from one subject to the next.

During that hour or so I don't remember saying much, but I did ask a number of questions. As we stood to leave Jerry said, "This was a wonderful conversation." I learned later that he told Mary I was a great conversationalist.

Skillful Listening Is The Key To Being A Great Conversationalist

The truth is that we did not have anything resembling a two-way conversation. It was a one-way conversation, with my asking questions.

One of the most important ingredients in listening is being genuinely interested in learning what the other person says. If you are not interested in what your partner says, something's wrong.

Comments

Listening authentically to another human takes a great deal of skill. If you are preoccupied or too tired to listen, you need to let your partner know and make arrangements to talk later.

Attempt to feel what your partner is feeling. Mastering the art of listening takes a lifetime of practice, but it starts with staying tuned in while your partner communicates.

Once this is accomplished, find and acknowledge the areas of agreement, define the areas of disagreement, respect one another's right to hold differing opinions, and seek solutions you both can embrace.

If you feel buried beneath an avalanche of words, take time out to repeat what you heard. Say something like, "What I heard is that you feel like I'm not paying attention to you and you want me to demonstrate that I really listen, is that right?" Repeating what you hear until your partner agrees with your perception takes time but is well worth the effort.

If you are preoccupied or too busy to listen to your partner, what is the underlying message? _____

_____

_____

_____

_____

What action would be good for you to take now?

_____

_____

_____

Affirmation   I Am Skilled At Listening.

References   A wonderful place to begin learning skillful listening is by reading Steven R. Covey's book, *The 7 Habits of Highly Effective People.*

Chapter 7

DON'T ESCALATE

Ken and Kate rarely quarrel, because things tend to get out of hand. When one of them brings something up, the other is quick to counter with something else. Pretty soon, dirty laundry is hauled up from the basement of their long but not very satisfying history together. Little is ever resolved, little is forgiven, and nothing is forgotten. That's why they don't allow themselves to express their feelings very often: it doesn't get them anywhere.

I know what it feels like. One day, during my first marriage, I arrived *Speak With Calm Words* home having forgotten that I had agreed to talk with my wife about our budget. Eventually, she reminded me and we began talking, but I was already on the defensive. The first thing I heard was an accusation that I wasn't making enough money and my impulse was to flee the scene. Actually, she didn't say I wasn't making enough money and to my knowledge didn't even believe it to be true. Somehow, I had added the implication.

Anyway, I became defensive and wanted to get away, but I forced myself to stay, to "hear her out," though I wasn't listening to what she was saying but to what I was afraid she might be saying. As the conversation continued I started moving away from the subject and instead began complaining that she was always complaining and that her complaining was the heart of this matter. Of course, it wasn't.

The heart of the matter was that I was uncomfortable negotiating a rigid budget and it was I, not she, who felt I wasn't bringing enough money home.

As I continued turning the attention away from the subject and toward her, both of us began to heat up. Soon, we were involved in a word-war that ended with me walking out of the room with a few chosen words.

Food For
Thought

Has something like this ever happened to you? Describe it _____

_____

_____

_____

_____

Do you know how to prevent it from happening again?

❑ YES   ❑ NO

Comments

Escalation occurs when a casual conversation turns into a serious discussion and then into a heated argument which erupts into a fight.

Some people use escalation out of frustration, and because it is the only way they know how to get their point across or to get their way.

Couples who have healthy and happy marriages know how to keep this from happening; they practice de-escalating. First they tell their partners the truth about how they feel. They stay on the subject, keep their voices modulated, check out their assumptions, and establish rules for mutual disagreement. Some typical rules might be:

- Discuss one subject only; schedule other subjects that come up for later discussion.

- Agree upon the time and place for discussing a volatile issue: e.g., not in the bedroom, and never when others are present.

- Validate one another's feelings; there are no "wrong" feelings.

- Find "the grain of truth" in statements with which there is disagreement.

- Seek solutions that are win-win.

I Practice The Art Of De-escalation.   *Affirmation*

If you do not know how to prevent your discussions   *References*
from escalating, you will find several suggestion in
DON'T ESCALATE, Section 3, p. 180.

Chapter 8

CARE FOR THAT INJURY

W e were playing war, Luke and I. We both carried sticks, imagining them to be guns. Old
army caps were our only real uniform; the rest was
supplied by our imaginations. We ran, then crawled,
then hid behind trees, periodically
peeking around them while firing; *We can't escape our past,*
then ducking. We gave and took *but we can resolve it.*
orders from one another, some
shouted, some whispered. We were courageous heroes
successfully annihilating the imagined enemy.
Moving more like cats than kids, we went from backyard to backyard until we came to a wall. It was stuc-
co-like, painted white with a rounded-off top. How
we scaled it, I don't remember.

I went first and made it. On the other side I waited
for Luke to slide over the top and drop to the ground
without being seen or shot. I was crouching, trying to
stay out of the enemies' sights while waiting for him
to appear. Looking back now, I don't remember seeing him come over the top; my only memory was
that as he slid down the wall, a protruding nail
caught his arm pit and tore it open. I remember hearing both the tearing and Luke's screaming. My most
vivid memory is of raw flesh and yellowish fat. As
Luke continued to scream, I ran to get a mother — I
don't remember whose. Our war game had ended in
tragedy. We were six years old.

Nearly fifty years later, my wife Linda and I were in
France visiting Monet's home and garden. We arrived
just as the grounds were opening and were among the
first visitors of the day. We like to arrive early in order
to miss the crowd. We had a couple of weeks left on

our vacation, and we were in no hurry. We sauntered through the Impressionist's home. It was quaint and wonderful. The yellow kitchen reminded me of some other kitchen I had been in, but I couldn't remember just when or where.

Outside, next to the house, a few chickens were clucking and scratching in a cordoned-off area. The scene reminded me of thousands of identical scenes at the Minnesota farm where I was raised. The garden was planted in rows, making it possible to touch the plants or pull a flower closer in order to enjoy its fragrance. We visited the store where huge reproductions of Monet's paintings and photographs of the artist covered the walls. Smaller versions were available for purchase. I was especially delighted to see photographs of Monet walking and sitting in the very garden we had just left.

In order to see the stream and ponds which served as subjects for some of his most beloved paintings, we walked down an alley-like pathway between two eight-foot walls. I was happy and relaxed. I was on vacation with the wife of my dreams, with no phone calls to receive or return. At the moment it happened, I don't remember if we were talking, joking, or just walking in silence, but fire suddenly painted my body from within. It was an unexpected shock, one that amazed but didn't frighten me.

I have this reaction every time I come across such a sight. It is beyond my control. If I spot the nail at a distance, it doesn't happen. I can walk up to it or pass it with little notice and no adrenaline. It's just when I'm taken by surprise at seeing one that the reaction explodes within me.

I knew instantly what had happened and why. What had happened was that a huge dose of adrenaline had been released and was now racing through my body. I was suddenly fully awake and alert, more awake at that moment than I had been in months.

Adrenaline is the body's way of signaling danger. It allows us the momentary hyper-speed and strength we need to run from the enemy or to stand and fight. I also knew why adrenaline was shooting through me on that quiet, harmless path near Monet's garden. My body and mind flawlessly remembered the terror I experienced of seeing and hearing the tearing open of my friend's underarm nearly 50 years earlier.

I reported the incident to my wife. Moments later we were walking near the stream, the ponds, and the bridges captured in Monet's paintings. The adrenaline and its effects had faded. However, I knew that adrenaline would return again and again for the rest of my life when I am surprised by a rusty nail sticking out of a wall. It happened just now as I wrote of it.

Whenever this happens to me, I talk myself through it. I remind myself that during that childhood war-game I was "emotionally injured" even though I was not the one who'd been physically wounded. The injury has not debilitated me, but just as getting hit on a black and blue wound hurts every time, so this life-long emotional bruise responds to each "hit."

My emotional injury is merely inconvenient. Some people have received blows that still debilitate them, sending them into panic attacks, neurotic impulses, or worse.

My Trigger is _____   *Food For*
                                                     Thought
_____

_____

_____

My Reactions are _____

_____

_____

_____

My Partner's Trigger is _____

_____

_____

My Partner's Reactions are _____

_____

_____

_____

Comments   A trigger is anything that initiates a Pavlovian response; i.e., a knee-jerk, unconscious, often unwanted but automatic reaction.

A person may have many triggers. Setting off one trigger can cause a chain reaction of unforeseen and unwanted consequences.

Reward the willingness to explore and resolve triggering incidents with patience and understanding. There is no greater gift you can give yourself or your partner than patience and understanding without judgment or blame.

Affirmation   I Know My Triggers.

References   See *CARE FOR THAT INJURY*, in *Section 3, p. 181.*

Chapter 9

FEED YOUR SOUL

S teve was rich and famous but, while pointing to his chest, he said, "I am hollow in here." I asked him what he meant by that. "I have a lot, but it's not enough," he replied.

Even though he had pointed within, at first I thought he meant that he had a heartfelt need for more material things and greater accomplishments. But he said he was not interested in making another million or seeing himself on TV again. He wanted to be happy.

Leaving the spiritual component out of relationships is the equivalent of owning a car but refusing to put fuel into it.

If I drew a cartoon of Steve's soul, it would be skinny as a rail. On the outside he was a fat cat. On the inside he was famished and starving to death. He had under-nourished his soul.

Philosophically, Steve was agnostic. He believed humans were advanced monkeys and thought of religion as institutionalized superstition and "something that appeals mostly to women." We laughed at my calling him "a spiritual bulimic," after he said that religious services "make me sick."

I suggested a spiritual program to build up the strength of his inner man. This program had worked for me and now it is working for him.

But before I give you the menu I handed him, I want to say a few things about spiritual nourishment in general.

As we all know, nourishment is essential to life, but we must feed the soul as well as the body and the ego. To live wisely we must nourish ourselves properly in order to construct a reliable foundation on which to build our future. Nourishing our soul is a certain sign of being on the right path.

Comments

When we gorge on activities, people, work,

accomplishments, and diversions, all of which are good when done in moderation, denying ourselves inspiration, comfort, relaxation, and energy-producing enthusiasm, we may soon find ourselves, like Steve, runnin' on empty. Overdoing it in one area prevents us from fueling ourselves properly in other areas. Balance and moderation are two critical keys.

The pace at which most of us are presently living, overcrowding our lives with people, activities and things, may enrich us materially, vocationally, and egotistically but impoverishes us spiritually.

Frantic to keep up, to get and stay ahead, to live life fully, to keep pace with our magnificent machines and the glut of information they bring, we are deluded into thinking that there's not enough time to stop and smell the roses. We are racing toward the end of our lives trying to cram in as much as possible before it's too late. As our pace continues to accelerate, we move into overwhelm. At breakneck speed we tend to make quick and poor decisions, to be defensive and cranky.

A significant part of being a healthy, loving partner is to take care of ourselves as if we were the primary care-giver of a god.

In order to be well-nourished and healthy, we need to access health-producing knowledge and practices. There is no easier way to strengthen our entire psychological make-up than by participating in spiritual practices that have proven effective. By this, I mean something slightly different than just being uplifted and inspired intellectually and emotionally. I'm suggesting becoming acquainted with the deepest core of our being.

Spiritual practices can be compared to the Special Olympics. There are enormous differences between the Olympics and the Special Olympics. To name one, in the Olympics there are only a few winners but many losers. In the Special Olympics there are only winners and no losers. Everyone who participates in any way wins. Anyone who gives money, time, ideas, organizational skill, who drives, sells tickets, as well as each contender, wins. It is a pure example of a win-win arrangement. So are spiritual practices.

As well-intentioned as they may be, religions tend to form boundaries that embrace believers and wall off others. Insiders can be compared to the winners, while outsiders are often viewed as potential insiders.

If you have never participated in spiritual practices, or if you have been avoiding them, now is the time to engage your higher Self. Your higher Self is the central core of yourself. It is that part of you which is one step below God Almighty, wise beyond belief, and the actual creator of your earth-bound life.

People in healthy relationships have achieved some degree of spiritual wholeness. They have done so by feeding their souls. Please join them.

When was the last time you took time to nourish your Soul? _____ *Food For Thought*

Do you know what activity or activities would nourish your Soul best?

❏ YES   ❏ NO

I Practice Spiritual Wholeness Through Self-nourishment. *Affirmation*

See *FEED YOUR SOUL* in *Section 3, p. 185.* *References*

Chapter 10

WRITE THAT LETTER

A 28-year-old man named Larry came to see me as the result of a terrifying experience. A few days earlier, he had been making love to his fiancé Heather, when all of a sudden, without warning, he froze. He couldn't respond to Heather's panic; he described himself as being catatonic. It scared both of them nearly to death. Within his "frozen cocoon" as he called it, he was alive, terrified, and thinking.

This was not something he did. It was something that had happened to him. It took several minutes before he recalled a 20-year-old memory. As soon as he remembered it, Larry began to recover. Meantime, Heather was in near panic, thinking that he was dying. As she was thinking of calling 911, Larry began to recover.

What had happened was that some touch, some word, something which Larry could not recall had triggered the repressed memory of his uncle's molesting him when he was eight years of age. As he was raping Larry, he whispered in his ear, "This is our secret. Never tell anyone." At some level, Larry had agreed.

When Larry was ten, his uncle died. At the funeral he had a great deal of trouble to keep from smiling. That was the day he buried the memory of the molestation.

I encouraged Larry to join a group for victims of molestation, but he refused. Then, I suggested that he write his dead uncle a letter. Even today, I don't know what was in that letter but a week later Larry read me his opening line. It started, "Dear Uncle John."

I was astonished. "Is Uncle John really 'dear' to you?" I questioned.

"No," he said, "but I'm a good Catholic and I cannot write down what I really wish to call him." I encouraged him to do so, to let it all hang out.

Because it is inappropriate to share the content of such letters, other than his salutation, I have no idea what he eventually wrote. I lost contact with Larry, but sometime later a friend of his, who apparently knew nothing of this incident, casually mentioned that he and Heather had married and were doing fine.

Food For Thought
Has anyone in your life caused you misery? _____

If you cannot tell him or her, are you willing to write a letter if you do not have to send it or show it to anyone, ever? _____

Comments
How can we get rid of our rage? How do we uncover thoughts and feelings that we formerly repressed? If we are not allowed to rage, what can we do with our anger? One of the most helpful, healing, and non-threatening ways I know is to write therapeutic letters.

A therapeutic letter is a letter I write but never send.

A therapeutic letter is a letter I write but never, under any circumstances, show to anyone.

A therapeutic letter is to my mind and memory what throwing up is to my stomach when I have eaten something that has made me sick.

A therapeutic letter is a controlled way of "venting my spleen," of "getting it out into the open," of finally "saying what I've always wanted to say."

A therapeutic letter is self-education. While writing, and later while reading it, I learn what I forgot that I forgot; I even learn what I experienced before I was able to think with words.

Affirmation
I Write Therapeutic Letters & Express My Fears & Rage To Skilled Listeners Before Expressing Them To My Partner.

References
See *WRITE THAT LETTER, Section 3, p. 192.*

Chapter 11

TELL THE TRUTH

R uth said she came to see me because she was con-templating taking a new job and she found it impossible to broach the subject with Raymond, her husband. Accepting a new job would entail dislodging her family, something she knew her husband did not want. As I listened, it became obvious she had already decided to take the job.

The real reason she had come was to practice her lines and drum up the courage to tell him. I asked her why she was so reluctant to discuss the matter with Ray.

She said, "I'm not accustomed to asking directly for what I want. I usually test the waters and when I feel it is safe, I mention it, usually humorously."

I encouraged her to bring the matter up, say what she wanted, and listen to Ray's response with compassion.

She called the next day to tell me that her husband had exploded. "He resisted, even threatened divorce."

"What are you going to do?" I asked.

"I'm not sure."

In the long run Ruth took the job, and Ray and their two children remained in their home for another year until the oldest graduated from high school. By that time Ray had secured a transfer from his company and he and the youngest joined Ruth.

Ruth's reluctance to be "up front" with her wants and desires is common. When we feel that "our truth" is going to cause a hassle or that we will meet with great resistance, we often choose to remain silent or manipulate until we get our way. Usually, we postpone the moment of truth until we cannot delay any longer, and then we must deal with the question, "Why didn't you tell me sooner so I could better prepare for it?"

Food For Thought Have you ever found it difficult or impossible to tell your partner the truth about something? _____

Is there anything that you have withheld from telling your partner that your partner needs to know?_____

Why? _____

_____

_____

_____

Are you ready to tell the truth now? _____

A Suggestion Before doing so, meet with a trusted friend or counselor and do what Ruth did: practice your lines and drum up the courage to tell your partner. You could write out what you wish to say, or you might want to practice your lines in front of a mirror or into a tape recorder.

Reluctance may prevent you from reporting your truth. You may decide to under-report it by leaving out some details or down-playing how you truly feel. You may choose to over-report it by being over-dramatic in order to solicit a response, or to play the martyr and receive a sympathetic ear; i.e., by manipulation.

Lying, whether with words, silence, gestures, or emotions, is a sure sign of unfaced trouble. Research has proven that unfaced problems heighten the possibility of disconnection and divorce. Instead, tell the truth skillfully and let the chips fall where they may. It will set you free!

Affirmation I Tell The Truth As Soon As Possible.

References See *TELL THE TRUTH, Section 3, p. 196.*

Chapter 12

LEARN ABOUT ONE ANOTHER

J anet had struggled with relationships most of her life. According to her, their father was harder on her than he was on her brothers. Her brothers were mean to her while treating one another well. In school, she felt that the teachers hated her because she asked embarrassing questions, and other students were jealous because she was smart. In business, she was always blamed for other employees' mistakes, and in marriage (she'd had three husbands) she was the victim of conniving men.

We had many conversations about her problems, and in no instance did Janet ever accept responsibility for anything that had happened to her. Someone else was always to blame, and nothing could be done about it because it was all hopeless. She was dedicated to a negative, pessimistic point of view.

One day, with great enthusiasm, she called to tell me about a book she'd just read. It was *Secrets About Men Every Woman Should Know* by Barbara DeAngelis, Ph.D. (Dell, New York, 1993). Janet said this book had taught her more about herself and about men, why she was the way she was and men were the way they were, than any other book she'd read or course she'd taken.

The opposite sex sometimes seems like a different species altogether.

Janet still struggles with relationships but her attitude is much improved. She attends group therapy sessions weekly and continues to read about the seemingly different planets that men and women inhabit, a concept made famous in another wonderful book, *Men*

"I wish someone would explain myself to me."
ELIZABETH IN
A WOMAN OF INDEPENDENT MEANS.

Are From Mars Women Are From Venus, by John Gray. Janet typifies most of us in that cleaning up our act often requires both new information and therapy.

Recently she told me, "The greatest discovery I've made is that men are not women with masculine bodies."

Food For Thought   Instigate an educational adventure by reading three books, one written by a man, two by women. Over the years I've read dozens of books on the subject of gender, and I've gotten more down-to-earth clarity about the similarities and differences between women and men from these three books than from all the others:

- *Men, Women, and Aggression*, Anne Campbell (Basic Books, 1993)
- *Men Are From Mars Women Are From Venus*, John Gray, Ph.D. (Harper Collins, 1992)
- *You Just Don't Understand: Women & Men in Conversation*, Deborah Tannen (Morrow, 1990)

People in successful relationships make a continuing, conscious effort to understand their partners in terms of their gender and as unique individuals. We never stop learning about one another. It is as if we were in an on-going class called "Understanding What My Partner Is Really Like."

Affirmation   I Am A Student Of Both Sexes.

References   See *LEARN ABOUT ONE ANOTHER* in *Section 3, p. 197.*

Chapter 13

GIVE 10s

J ay was the kind of guy who ranked women on a scale of one to ten and was proud of his high standards. Only movie stars got a ten from Jay, and very few of them at that. No wonder he was never satisfied with the women he dated. They just couldn't measure up.

"What grade do you think you'd get?" I asked him. Jay was anything but humble. "At least an eight. More likely a nine."

"I'd give you a ten," I said.

"You would?"

"Yes," I said. "I give everyone a ten."

If we are to have peace of mind which leads to peaceful relationships, it is helpful to grade one another as if we were all participants in the Special Olympics. During the Special Olympics, the participants are given perfect scores just for showing up, ribbons pinned on their shirts and blouses for doing their best, and applause for the magnificent accomplishment of simply trying. When we adopt this attitude toward everyone, especially those with whom we are intimate, we will have greatly matured.

Dr. Harvell Hendricks is fond of saying that happily married couples remind themselves often that they are living with a wounded partner, and so is their partner.

Comments

Living day after day in relative harmony requires a belief that others are doing their best to "get along." This happens the moment we realize that all of us, given our own internal condition and taking into consideration everything we have been through both recently and during our lifetime, at every moment of every day, are constantly operating at our best.

Food For   When considering your part of your relationship
Thought   only, what grade would you give yourself? _____

What grade would you give your partner? _____

Affirmation   I Give High Grades To My Partner.

Chapter 14

RECONNECT

M y primary relationship is with my wife Linda. All other relatives, friends, and loyalties come after ours. One of the ways we retain this primacy is by staying in contact. When she is home, I call her once or twice each day, often just to say "hello."

Linda is a flight attendant. She works the international routes only and flies from San Francisco to Australia, China, France, Great Britain, Hawaii, Hong Kong, Japan, Korea, and so forth.

She is away from home between one night and five or six each trip. If she is in Hawaii, I call her or she calls me. When she is elsewhere, I fax her every other day. My faxes consist of common occurrences, copies of letters I've written or received, and other bits and pieces of what's happening.

I love to send those faxes as much as she loves receiving them. For Linda, it reassures her that I love her, that she is on my mind, and she is not missing something important or being left out of the day-to-day happenings.

When you are apart for a few hours, how do you stay connected to your partner?_____ *Food For Thought*

_____

When you are apart for a few days, how do you stay connected to your partner?_____

_____

When you are apart for a few weeks, how do you stay connected to your partner?_____

_____

If you are so busy or caught up in your own thoughts and plans that when you see your partner, you immediately launch into what's on your mind without so much as a hello, consider the example of chimpanzees. Even when they are separated for only a matter of minutes, they reunite. Their vocalizing, touching, stroking, grooming, making eye contact, and gesturing apparently bring comfort and give reassurance of safety and belonging.

Research, conducted by observation, surveys, and interviews with couples who have long, happy relationships, reveals that they bond and rebond nearly every time they come back together.

Affirmation   I Rebond Often.

Chapter 15

SAY, "THANKS"

P eter said, "I know Fran loves me, but I don't think she *appreciates* me." Fran disagreed. "Of course I appreciate you," she said. "Whatever gave you the idea I don't?"

Peter was just waiting for her to ask. "I fix your car; I pick things up for you; last week I painted the bathroom."

Fran had her own list. "I cook breakfast and dinner every day; I clean the house."

"I work; I'm the breadwinner."

"Wait a minute!" I stopped them before the competition got out of hand. "Let's shift gears. For a minute, forget your own contributions and focus only on thanking one another for doing things you appreciate."

Pretty soon Fran and Peter were outdoing one another, this time with gratitude.

Sometimes, I recommend that partners practice this technique. It's not only a skilled thing to do, it also often reveals much deeper problems.

Several weeks later, Fran and Peter came back to see me. They said that they now found it impossible to compliment one another or even to say "Thank you," not because the other person didn't deserve it but because they were constantly angry.

Independently, they both had discovered that their internal voices were conducting a council meeting which consisted of a constant tirade against life and most others, sometimes even against themselves ("You are so stupid, Fran"; "You really are a jerk, Peter"; "Secretly, you're really mean, Fran").

Food For
Thought

I find it impossible to compliment my partner.

❏ YES   ❏ NO

Comments

Sometimes partners find it impossible to clean things up between them, because they carry within themselves so many unresolved fears and resentments. Often these resentments are credited to their partner but would be more appropriately directed inward. If this is true for you, seek help.

Affirmation

I Compliment My Partner And Say "Thank You" Often.

Chapter 16

GIVE DELIGHTFUL SURPRISES

M oses saw Lois pour the perfume he'd bought her down the drain. Convinced their relationship was over, he came to see me because he wanted "a shoulder to swear on."

"Don't you think you're jumping to conclusions?" I asked him.

"You're the one who told me to be sensitive to gestures and nuance," he responded.

When I next saw him, he was all smiles. "Lois was allergic to something in the perfume I bought her," he informed me.

A "conscious gift" is a present that the recipient likes. An "unconscious gift" is a present the giver likes and therefore, often mistakenly, thinks the recipient will enjoy. Happily married couples give time and consideration to their gift-giving and are thereby skilled at giving conscious presents.

Comments

When your partner points out something he or she likes, or says, "I wish I had one of those," make a note of it below. Over the years your list will grow and your partner will be delighted rather than disappointed. The overall result will be that each time you need an idea for a gift, you will have a list of things truly wanted.

Food For Thought

1. _____

2. _____

3. _____

4. _____

5._____

6._____

Affirmation   I Give Conscious Gifts & Unexpected, Delightful
Surprises.

References   See *GIVE DELIGHTFUL SURPRISES, Section 3, p. 200.*

Chapter 17

SAY, "YOU'RE GREAT!"

Nathan and I were bragging about our wives. He said that every so often his wife says something like: "Nate, I want you to know how much I appreciate your willingness to work. I appreciate that you spend three hours on the freeway every day. I also appreciate how much money you make and bring home. Thank you."

I told him I'd never heard someone say such a wonderful thing to his or her partner.

I could hardly wait to try it out on my wife. I meant every word I said, too. Linda loved it. Your partner will too.

Do you brag about your partner to others? _____   *Food For*
Thought
If not, why not? _____

_____

_____

Write down the characteristics you treasure in your partner_____

_____

_____

_____

_____

Read the list to your partner.

Happily married folks are always bragging about one another. Couples who have healthy relationships compliment one another and say "thank you" often.

I Acknowledge My Partner To Others.   *Affirmation*

Chapter 18

SHARE YOUR STUFF

B uff is a typical yuppie. He dresses well, drives a BMW, and exudes self-confidence. When he was forty, he proposed to Melissa and she accepted. Then, a few weeks before the wedding, Buff asked to see me privately — he was adamant about not wanting Melissa to know of our meeting — he needed to talk about his fear of sharing.

"This is the first time for both of us," he began, "and I want it to be the last. Melissa is the woman I've dreamed about my entire life. I feel good, light, and happy whenever we're together. We communicate well, have fun spontaneously, and I've never been happier."

"Then why are you so miserable?" I asked him.

"You'll laugh," he said.

"I don't think so."

"It's my Beemer," he said.

"Your car?" I asked.

Buff told me he was the youngest of four brothers and when he was growing up they always teased him by "stealing" (borrowing and hiding) his toys, clothes, and possessions. They also stole food from him. For example, if he turned his head away from his plate his piece of chicken would disappear. Their parents would scold them but that was the extent that correction ever went.

All this teasing made Buff distrustful of his brothers and now, against his will and better judgment, he had the same feelings about Melissa. He didn't want her to drive his car, enter his apartment, have access to his money, or monopolize his time. He found that his first reaction to sharing was an internal cringe. I asked him to explain what he meant. He said he felt like a scared turtle pulling into his shell for protection whenever he was required to share.

It seemed obvious to me, but Buff could not accept the idea that his childhood experiences were overriding his feelings for Melissa. "It might lead to a possible solution," I suggested, "if you told her everything you'd told me." However, Buff said he was too embarrassed to do that.

A few weeks later, he brought Melissa to see me. In my presence, and with great reluctance and genuine embarrassment, he told her the story.

Melissa responded by saying, "Don't you think I've known this from the beginning?"

They went on to talk about other things. I remained quiet, thinking that now that Buff had placed his cards on the table face up, things would be fine between them.

They have now been married three years. Recently, I ran into Buff at a store and asked him how he was doing. Still embarrassed about it, he said that he still has qualms about sharing but so far his wife has never taken advantage of him or stolen anything.

"I still won't let her drive the Beemer, though," he joked.

Food For Thought

Are you good at sharing? ❑ YES ❑ NO

If not, can you remember when your reluctance began? Perhaps you are still being defensive even though there is no present threat.

Are you willing to share your thoughts and feeling with your partner? ❑ YES ❑ NO

If not, are you willing to share them with anyone?

❑ YES ❑ NO

Who?_____

Whether it is time, food, space, money, or the TV *Comments*
clicker, some folks are not skilled at sharing. When
they were young, they may have been denied love or
sustenance. Their families may have been financially
embarrassed. Impending disaster may have been
regularly discussed at family gatherings.

They may have experienced poverty so deeply that
saving, hoarding, and protecting became habitual. It
may be such a simple thing as having grown up in a
large family where they needed to protect their food
from older brothers who teased them by snatching it
during meals.

People who are poor at sharing make difficult partners. Sometimes such people find one another and
reinforce each other's habits. Marriage requires a great
deal of sharing. Being "happily married" implies
sharing nearly everything.

I Am Good At Sharing. *Affirmation*

Chapter 19

TAKE TIME TO BE ALONE

While raising her family, Joan had gotten used to sublimating her desires. She also felt it was her duty to be on call twenty-four hours a day — and she had been for years. Even deciding to take care of her own needs wasn't easy. She felt guilty, selfish and as though she was abandoning her family, even though no one was complaining.

One day while participating in a discussion group for women, a memory surfaced. When she was a child, her younger brother, David, had come home from school while their mother was away having her hair done. David took advantage of the opportunity to use his bed as a trampoline. He catapulted off, hit his head on a table, and opened up a deep cut. He held a towel to his head until their mother returned. When she did, she drove David to the emergency room to get stitches.

The part that Joan recalled was the furious way her father had denounced their mother for not being home, which, in his estimation, would have prevented the accident from happening.

Joan, who was only about seven or eight at the time, remembered that he had accused her of being selfish and a poor mother. It was at that moment that Joan learned her first lesson in motherhood, a sick and distorted form of motherhood where the mother's needs always come last.

Today, Joan is still hardly ever alone. "It doesn't feel right," she says. When her children are in school and her husband is at work, she busies herself talking with friends on the phone. The only time she spends alone is when she visits the bathroom and sometimes when she is cooking.

"Something's wrong," she said to me. "I don't know why I'm so afraid to be alone."

As mentioned above, Joan joined a women's group that meets weekly with a family psychologist. She tells me that she has discussed her fears with the group, but has not yet come to grips with the totality of why even the thought of being alone makes her uncomfortable.

Food For Thought   How much time do you spend alone for the sole purpose of nourishing yourself? _____

If you don't spend enough time alone, why not? __
_____

What do you most like to do when you're alone?
_____

Comments   Everyone needs a vacation now and then. Perhaps you could use an hour or two break from your partner, family, or household each week. Schedule time alone just as you would schedule a date. Write it down, and keep the appointment.

Healthy partners take care of themselves by spending time by themselves, not as a way of avoiding one another but as a way of recharging their batteries.

Being alone is a gift we give ourselves. It is a way of being nice to ourselves. It gives us time to either do nothing or to discover how we truly feel about something or someone. Taking time to be alone is not selfish-indulgence as Joan's father wrongly believed. He had selfishness and self-love confused.

Affirmation   I Take Time To Be By Myself.

References   See *TAKE TIME TO BE ALONE, Section 3, p. 201.*

Chapter 20

ESTABLISH LIFE GOALS

S ome time ago, Sarah Nolan (her real name) guided me though an exercise to help me formulate a Mission Statement for *The Alliance for Educational Development*, the non-profit corporation I head.

A significant part of the exercise was to focus on what I personally (not just professionally, although that is a part of it) wanted to do with the remainder of my life. What I had not realized was that I had already determined my life's goal, but I didn't know I knew it.

My personal mission is to live a *A Mission Statement* balanced life between family, work and play, and to leave my world in better condition than I found it.

I learned this from my mother.

I remember moving from a small house on McDuff Street in Los Angeles to a larger place a few blocks away. I had been transporting boxes and things all day. When I returned to McDuff for the last time to pick up a few remaining items, I found my mother on her knees scrubbing the kitchen floor. I asked, "Why are you doing that?"

She said, "When we moved in here this place was dirty. I want to leave it cleaner than I found it." At the time I thought what she was doing was a needless waste of time and I told her so.

I did not realize until years later that her simple statement set me on my life's goal.

What do you want out of life? _____ *Food For Thought*

Are you on a path that will allow you to eventually achieve your goal? ❑ YES   ❑ NO

If not, what adjustments do you need to make? ____

_____

_____

_____

_____

Comments   When we're fulfilled, we are well on our way to becoming happy.

One of the greatest gifts we can give ourselves is this clarity.

The most unhappy people I encounter during counseling sessions are those who, even though they may be forty years old or older, still don't know what they want to do with their lives.

Here are a couple of simple ways that will help you to determine your life's goals:

1) Pretend that you have only six months to live. What will you do and what will you not do? (To be sure, we cannot live continually with this thought in mind because long-term planning is necessary. However, this simple exercise will help clarify and prioritize things.)

2) Make a list of one-hundred things you wish to do before you die. There are no restrictions to this list. It can contain things of varying importance. For example, one desire might be to wake up early, walk or drive to a particular spot, and watch the sunrise. Another, might be to graduate from college or to build your own house.

Affirmation   I Know What I Want Out Of Life.

References   See *ESTABLISH LIFE GOALS, Section 3, p. 201.*

Chapter 21

PREPARE FOR DEATH

We may be able to prepare very well for our own deaths, but we can't prepare adequately for the deaths, of our loved ones.

There are several ways to get in touch with your feelings and thoughts about your death. One of these self-educating techniques is to pretend that you are being honored at a "This is Your Life" type of event. A dear friend of yours stands and gives a toast in your honor. What your friend says is:

Food For Thought

_____

_____

_____

_____

_____

_____

Those who have studied happy people suggest that they are able to live fully because they have accepted their mortality. "Accepting your own death" means that it is genuinely OK with you that your physical body dies. If you have not already accepted this reality, writing your own obituary is one way to start on the path toward acceptance.

Comments

I Am Preparing For My Own Death.

Affirmation

See *PREPARE FOR DEATH, Section 3, p. 202.*

References

Chapter 22

LIVE FULLY

Here is the other side of the coin described in Chapter 20, where we looked at what you want out of life. They differ in that Chapter 20 is about gaining clarity about life while this chapter is about making plans, identifying the steps needed, and having the courage to take those steps.

I enjoy speculating about dying and the immediate after-life. One of my favorite fantasies is that I have stepped out and away from my old, decrepit physical body and I'm standing before The Almighty — which, by the way, I consider to be the single safest place in existence.

The Almighty says, "George, my son. Welcome back home. By the way, what did you learn while on earth?"

With that, I evaluate what I've been up to lately. In this fantasy, one of the saddest things would be to arrive before The Almighty and have to report that despite the fact that I could have done it, fear kept me stuck in some old pattern or form of work.

This fantasy has served me well over the years as a motivator. It prods me when I become fearful. It allows me to distance myself just far enough from my physical body and its protective ego to remind me that it is important to take chances, to live my dream-life and not leave my dreams lying on the table.

The fantasy has served me so well, I invite you to participate in it and see what happens.

Food For
Thought What would your life be like if you were living at your full potential?_____

_____

_____

_____

_____

Comments It is unrealistic and, besides, it would be exhausting to live every single waking moment of the day to our full potential. However, most of us can accomplish more than we are currently doing.

Affirmation I Am Living Life To Its Fullest.

References See *LIVE FULLY, Section 3, p. 206.*

Chapter 23

ENABLE THE NEEDY

W e've all seen old movies in which early Americans gathered to help one another solve individual or community problems. I remember one where the women did the cooking while the men did the building, and in one day the community built a church. That kind of community "do-gooding" is still alive today, but because the projects and the forms and forums are different, they are not always recognized.

Happy people report that they are involved in volunteer activities. They are so healthy that they reach out beyond their own needs.

Their involvement goes beyond their immediate and extended family, and the activities range from A to Z.

When we spend all our time on ourselves, riveted in place while staring at our own navels, we are slowly suffocating ourselves.

According to Peter E. Drucker, "In the early 1990's, about a million organizations were registered in the United States as nonprofit or charitable organizations." Most of these organizations welcome volunteers. Becoming an active volunteer adds value to life.

I'm good at _____   *Food For Thought*

_____

I can best serve my community by _____

_____

I Am Community-Minded.   *Affirmation*

See *ENABLE THE NEEDY, Section 3, p. 208*   *References*

Section 2

27 EXERCISES TO PRACTICE WITH YOUR PARTNER

Chapter 24

ESTABLISH RULES

Jules and Vivian had been married about five years. However, when it came to important decisions, both admitted that they always ended up wanting something different.

"Even when a marriage is made in Heaven, the maintenance work has to be done on earth."

I asked them to demonstrate one of their discussions.

As I listened it became clear that they approached problem-solving as if it were a "winner take all" free-for-all street fight. Verbally, they went out of control.

Frequently in couples' counseling, the task of the counselor is to act as a coach. Often, the counselor is a referee. With Jules and Vivian, I shared seven rules (below) which will keep a discussion from escalating into a fight. They didn't have any rules.

Comments

I met with them four more times. They came to the realization that using rules for household discussions kept the pot from boiling over.

People skilled at conflict-management (that is, those who discuss things rather than argue or fight) do the following:

Food For Thought

1. Within 24 hours of the conflict, they arrange a meeting to discuss the issue.
2. They discuss one subject at a time.
3. They report their feelings first (sometimes, that's all they report). And, they report only two or three feelings at a time.
4. No violence is present. (Violence comes in three forms: verbal, emotional, and physical.) There is no intimidation or threat of intimidation. Belittling, sarcasm, and raw, vicious criticism are absent.

5. They compliment one another and validate one another's view points. ("Yes, I see your point." "That's a great idea." "Thank you for being honest about how you feel." "I think you've just come up with the solution.")
6. They complete their discussions in skilled ways. (See Chapter 26)
7. They stay constructively involved by practicing these skills, and they seek outside help when they realize they have reached an impasse.

Affirmation   We Are Skilled At Solving Problems.

References   See *ESTABLISH RULES, Section 3, p. 209.*

Chapter 25

CREATE HEALTHY BOUNDARIES

F red and Sarah had been married only a year when they came to see me. Fred complained, "Sarah has taken over my life." By that he meant that, despite his increasingly vehement objections, she continued to volunteer him for odd jobs for friends, make appointments for him, and arrange social events without ever consulting him.

She readily admitted doing everything he accused her of doing. However, she could not understand why Fred didn't appreciate her serving as their social secretary — a job her mother had done in her family.

Neither one had heard of the term "healthy boundaries."

I mentioned several examples: Borrowing things that belong to others without asking permission. Walking into a room and taking over the radio, stereo, or TV that is already being used. Walking into the bathroom when the door is closed. Taking food off someone's plate.

In other words, we respect their rights just as we expect them to respect our rights.

Prior to our next appointment, they read a brief but brilliant book on the subject by Anne Katherine, *Boundaries: Where You End and I Begin*. Parkside Publishing Corporation, 1991.

I recommend her book to you.

Have you ever had one of your boundaries violated?

❏ YES   ❏ NO

If so, when and in what way? _____

_____

Does your partner violate any of your boundaries?

_____

Do you violate your partner's boundaries. (You might want to ask him/her.) _____

What are you willing to do about this now? _____

_____

_____

_____

Affirmation   We Have Established And We Respect Healthy Boundaries.

Chapter 26

LEAVE WITH SKILL

My wife and I had gone to dinner with Bill and Kimberly a few times. We were both a little uncomfortable being with them, but we couldn't put our finger on just why.

Sometime later, I attended a class at the Denver University given by Howard Markman, Ph.D. and Dr. Clifford Notarius, Ph.D. It was there that I first heard of "exiting." As soon as I heard about it, I knew why we had been uneasy with Bill and Kimberly.

It seemed that both always wanted to have the last word. And, the last word usually was some comment that expressed at least a slight bit of disapproval, usually couched in the form of a tease or a joke. At times, we even laughed, but after a while it became old. We found ourselves eating with them less and less and, now, not at all.

"Exiting" simply means the way we conclude a discussion. Couples who are clumsy or destructive in the way they end their discussions (arguments or fights) divorce at significantly higher rates than those who exit skillfully.

A few examples of unskilled exiting are: verbally attacking my partner and walking away, withdrawing from the conversation, changing the subject, refusing to talk, using violent, controlling, or battering language such as, "You are the dumbest person on earth. All of our trouble is your fault."

A few examples of skilled exiting are: "I'm feeling overwhelmed. Let's take a break for an hour. I'll take responsibility for opening the discussion when we return." "We didn't settle this so we need to continue this discussion later. What is a good time for you?"

Comments

75

Are you skilled when it comes to ending a conversation? ❑ YES   ❑ NO

What could you do to improve? _____

_____

_____

_____

Is your partner skilled or unskilled when it comes to ending a conversation? ❑ YES   ❑ NO

What could he/she do to improve? _____

_____

_____

_____

Affirmation   We Practice Skilled Exiting.

Chapter 27

DON'T LIE

F our months after I had conducted her husband's funeral, Martha came to see me. She was extremely upset. My mind immediately suspected that I had said something during the memorial service that had angered her.

What I remembered saying was largely what she and her daughters told me about him; every word had been extremely positive. I distinctly remember her saying that her only regret was that, with her husband's death, their 40-year marriage had ended too soon.

Instead of talking, she sat and cried. She did so for a long time. When she finally spoke, it was with great difficulty. Stumblingly, she began, "It was all a lie. I've just found out something terrible about Jeffrey [her dead husband's name]. I've discovered that he had a secret savings account with $75,000 in it. Now as I look back, I wonder if anything he told me was true."

Her daughters had already gone through the positive possibilities; i.e., he was going to surprise her; he was saving it for her only; she should consider herself lucky that he didn't leave with a $75,000 debt; she should think only that his motivations were true to her, and so forth. However, not being able to verify which answer was true, she was left fretting over what felt to her as a 40-year betrayal.

Each time I tell this story, there are those who agree with her daughters. Often someone will laugh and say they wish this would happen to them. Their responses are, of course, funny at one level but they do not address the heart of the issue.

Martha feels that for some unknowable reason, her husband did not trust her, and now she is left to speculate, with dread, about the veracity of their entire marriage.

Food For Thought

Some secrets, such as a surprise party, are harmless when kept from our partner. People in the healing/helping professions — doctors, nurses, lawyers, clergy — are given confidential information that must not be relayed to their partner. Military secrets and information known by people such as Secret Service Agents must be respected. Retaining privacy in these matters does not constitute a violation of our most intimate relationships. However, nearly every other form of secret is a relationship-killer.

EXAMPLES OF DESTRUCTIVE SECRETS

1. A bank or savings account
2. A love affair
3. A disease or illness
4. Friends
5. Relationships — especially present relationships
6. A business partnership/deal
7. Relatives
8. Habits
9. Mail

Are you able to identify with Martha's plight?
❏ YES   ❏ NO

Are you currently keeping a destructive secret from your partner?   ❏ YES   ❏ NO

If you die with your secret intact and, following your death, your partner finds out the truth, will it leave your partner in a similar position as Jeffrey's secret left Martha?   ❏ YES   ❏ NO

Affirmation   We Do Not Have Destructive Secrets.

Resources   See *DON'T LIE, Section 3, p. 209.*

Chapter 28

KEEP YOUR WORD

Mark and Lyla met in high school, married during college, and were considering divorce before their fourth anniversary. Her reason for coming to talk was to stave off divorce. His reason was because he had "had it."

"Had what?" I asked. "I can't rely on her for anything," he exaggerated. "She never does what she says she will do. She's always late and then lies about what time she agreed to show up. She promises to do something, but does something different." By then he was becoming really angry. "She promised to put $500 in our account on Wednesday. That night she said she had but, the next Monday I found out that she had only put in $350 and did so on Friday, not Wednesday." He wanted to go on but I stopped him.

Turning to Lyla I said, "Would you like to say anything?" She said she didn't. I asked her if what Mark said was essentially true. She nodded yes.

Our conversation took many twists and turns. It ended with Lyla's promising to see a woman counselor and Mark's agreeing to postpone leaving, pending — "as long as she gets fixed."

Today they are divorced. To make a long story short, during her therapy, Lyla learned that she was dreadfully afraid of insensitive, bossy men and lied to them most of the time. In a subsequent phone call (for he refused to come in again), Mark admitted having those qualities, felt they were positive, and "the way men are suppose to be." He refused further therapy, and stated that he resented being asked to do so. After all, he intimated, she was the sick one, not he.

Food For
Thought

Does either Mark or Lyla remind you of yourself?

❑ YES   ❑ NO

If you are a frequent liar, do you know why and are you willing to address this problem now?

❑ YES   ❑ NO

Comments

Happy couples trust one another primarily because they have a track record of keeping their word or agreements. They can be trusted because they consistently tell the truth.

Smoking, heavy use of alcohol, huge intakes of sugar and animal fats, lack of sleep, presence of destructive stress, and constant anger can make one's physical body ill. Breaking agreements can ruin a healthy and loving relationship.

- Breaking agreements is one of the major killers of relationships.
- Breaking an agreement breeds mistrust.
- Breaking agreements is a controlling maneuver (manipulation).
- Breaking an agreement is never a meaningless activity.
- Breaking an agreement shows disrespect for your partner.
- Breaking agreements will always catch up with us.

Affirmation   We Seldom Break Agreements.

References   See *KEEP YOUR WORD, Section 3, p. 210.*

Chapter 29

DON'T PARENT YOUR PARTNER

Phil and Jill had been married nearly twenty years. They had two teen-age boys whom they described as "difficult and rude." Phil and Jill came to see me because they were no longer getting along and had been unable to understand why. Nearly at the moment I asked Jill to explain their situation, Phil interrupted her by making a minor correction to her story. Before she completed telling her side of the saga, he had interrupted or corrected her version several times. His demeaning her annoyed me.

When she finished, Phil began. She did to him exactly what he had done to her; i.e., interrupted or corrected his version several times. This also annoyed me.

It was clear that under their pleasant exteriors, claims of love, respect for, and devotion to one another, they were fighting for dominance.

These destructive habits and sexual harassment are identical in that both are about dominance and submission.

When I pointed this out, both denied it, followed immediately (actually at the same time) by each one's correcting the other. When I mentioned that they were interrupting one another, not allowing the other to speak, they denied it saying that I had misunderstood. At that point, I wished that I had recorded our conversation from its start.

I talked about the implications of always needing to be right, demanding verbal accuracy, and needing to have both the first and last word about everything. I reviewed the concepts I'm detailing in this chapter.

In order to finish, I had to hold my hand up several times and ask to be allowed to complete my remarks.

I met with them only twice. As of the moment, they continue their battle for dominance. I know this for two reasons. I observed them at a public event, both were correcting the other. I've also seen their boys who are imitating their parents. To say the least, these people are difficult to be with — they are finding it difficult to be with each other.

Food For Thought

Do you habitually interrupt or correct your partner?

❏ YES   ❏ NO

Do you habitually allow your partner to interrupt or correct you?   ❏ YES   ❏ NO

Do you try to teach your partner?

❏ YES   ❏ NO

If someone were to draw a cartoon of your relationship, what would it look like?

Our society places a huge premium on winning. It is not false to claim it as our Nation's most popular religion. This is true not only in sports and business but in religion, and education as well; in fact, the spirit of winning permeates many facets of our lives and affects all of them.

Being the first, the best, and the greatest are the bones for which the Top Dogs crave, fight, sacrifice, and sometimes die.

This chapter is not a naive call for us to give up our competitiveness. Like other knee-jerk impulses, our competitiveness is one of our innate impulses that enables us to survive.

What I am suggesting is that we control, direct, and compartmentalize our competitiveness. One of the compartments where competition must voluntarily be banned is in our intimate relationships within our households.

Competition, not unlike a pit bull, can turn and at any moment injure or viciously kill any relationship. Vicious competition is wrong. We need to stop deifying those who practice it. We must not allow it near our households.

Comments

We Seldom Correct, Instruct, Talk Over, Or Rudely Interrupt One Another —- Even In Private.

Affirmation

For more about Phil and Jill turn to *DON'T PARENT YOUR PARTNER* in *Section 3, p. 212.*

References

Chapter 30

DON'T ASSUME MIND READING

Victoria and Clark had been married only six months. They said they were having "communication problems." Among other things, their sex life had taken a nosedive. Each blamed the other.

The story was typical. Soon after they met, which had been two years before they married, they had a sex life which, according to both of them, was hot, torrid, and extremely fulfilling. They were able to give and receive sexual pleasure and feel loved easily. Things had cooled down over the next year and a half and, soon after they married, it nearly disappeared.

Clark admitted to not being as interested as he had been earlier, but took no blame for the "real cause" which he said was that Victoria refused to tell him what she wanted and did not want. He was constantly guessing incorrectly, and felt badly, but when he asked, Victoria would indicate that he should know — as he once did.

The first year and a half they had operated on newness and excitement fueled by idyllic romantic love. This is a relatively brief period of time when the chemicals are flowing freely and men often talk nearly as much as women, and in some cases, for the only time in their entire lives. The same elements are true for women and, for that period of time, they live in a protective shell where they are extremely receptive and forgiving, because they feel wanted and they feel that their partner can do no wrong.

Once these chemicals wear off, things cool down, and we're back to normal human functioning, misfiring often begins.

Victoria loved feeling the way she had earlier and was now disappointed that it wasn't continuing. A different type of love needed to be born. She had never so much as heard of a different form of love.

It turned out that both Victoria and Clark were secretly worried that they had fallen out of love. Instead, they now saw that something had been done to them against their wills. Their brains had shut off the chemicals that ignite pursuit and attraction, and turned on the chemicals that are less exciting but longer lasting.

Additionally, both were able to accept that their partner needs to be told, each time they make love, what is wanted.

A final illustration was also helpful. I said, "What if your partner comes home from work and you ask him/her what they want for dinner and they say, 'If you loved me enough, you would know.' What would you think?"

Immediately they saw how ludicrous it is to expect and demand that our partners be mind-readers rather than human beings.

Food For Thought

Do you "under-communicate" to your partner?

❏ YES   ❏ NO

Do you sometimes talk in outline form and expect your partner to fill in the blanks correctly?

❏ YES   ❏ NO

What would be a better approach? _____

_____

_____

Comments

Successful couples report that their partners' communications to them are accurate nearly all the time. They also report that they seldom have to fill in gaps or guess about their partners' communications.

Demanding that our partners be mind-readers is one of the most subtle killers of relationships. Making an assumption that our partners know what we are talking about without making ourselves clear, and expecting them to be mind-readers, is raw manipulation. Requiring our partners to be mind-readers puts them up on a pedestal from where it is easy to knock them off (put them down) when they don't get it right. This form of manipulation is exposed in sentences like these:

"If you really loved me you would have done ..." "You know how I feel." "It is more romantic when you just do so-and-so, rather than asking me what I want you to do." "I thought by now you would have understood what I wanted." "The reason you did that was ..." "I know what you had in mind."

We Do Not Demand That Our Partner Be A Mind-reader.   *Affirmation*

See *DON'T ASSUME MIND-READING, Section 3, p.212.*   *References*

Chapter 31

DON'T COMPETE

We're about to revisit Jules and Vivian. (See *Chapter 24, Establish Rules*, if you need to become reacquainted with them.)

It was clear that Jules and Vivian were more like boxers than lovers. They talked as if they were encountering an opponent. She would say something and his response had a slight edge to it. "We tried it your way and look at the mess it caused." "It turned out that you didn't know what you were talking about." "You always say that and you're wrong."

Her responses were equally sharp. "You made that decision and look what it led to." "You insisted we go there." "You forced me to agree."

Vivian claimed that Jules talked like her father. Her father owned a lumber company. According to her, he described himself as a tough guy who prided himself on being forthright and hard on his employees. "They always know where I stand and where they stand with me," she said he was fond of saying.

Unknown to her then, she hated the way her father treated everybody and the way he talked, but because of her authentic love for him (and the fact that she was his daughter and there was no escape), she put up with it.

When she met Jules, his manner and language resembled her father's and was familiar territory. That "familiar territory" along with her love for her father were a couple of the unconscious reasons why she was attracted to Jules.

Jules told a different but similar story about his father's manner and language.

When Jules and Vivian lived side by side on a daily basis, feeling there was no easy way out, they fought for dominance.

They didn't know how to do it but they had grown tired of this sort of low-life talk and were trying to stop it. However, they were trying to fight fire with fire.

I asked them to try two things:

1. Instead of trying to dominate one another over everything, agree about who will be in charge of a particular activity while the other person stays out of the way and takes on the role of helper.
2. The helper agrees not to criticize the way the other person has chosen to do the task.

I told them the story of the wall-papering job that my wife and I did together — an activity that for some has led directly to death and divorce.

We have never had a problem with wall-papering together because I, having never done it before, simply followed her lead. When she asked me to cut a piece a certain length or help her do something, I willingly cooperated.

She, with her almost professional knowledge, and her willingness to instruct me, combined with my willingness to cooperate, were the perfect ingredients.

They tried this approach but claimed they couldn't do it. What was actually true was that their habits went back so far and were so thoroughly ingrained that they refused to change. I also suspect that they felt that by changing they were giving into their partner who would reign over them triumphantly for the rest of their marriage.

I also invited them to try to clean up their language — language that both found offensive. They did not swear but their language was verbally sharp, cutting, and at times, downright cruel.

When these suggestions failed, I suggested that separately they seek counseling and deal with their distrust of one another as well as their family histories. They refused, and that was the last I've seen of them. Hopefully, they have sought professional help and have stopped competing with one another.

Are you in competition with your partner?

Food For Thought

❏ YES   ❏ NO

Do you correct one another's stories or jokes?

❏ YES   ❏ NO

Do you talk over your partner while your partner is talking?   ❏ YES   ❏ NO

Do you complete your partners' sentences?

❏ YES   ❏ NO

Do you add an appendix to nearly every statement your partner makes?   ❏ YES   ❏ NO

Do you find it difficult to compliment your partner with full-hearted sincerity?   ❏ YES   ❏ NO

If you have answered "yes" to any of these questions you are, perhaps, unknowingly, in competition with your partner. Often, this competition is about, who will be in charge of this relationship?

Comments

People who are psychologically healthy (folks who are mentally and spiritually together) and who are skilled at relationships (they discuss their differences rather than argue or fight about them) are not in relationship-competition. They see their partners more as colleagues who are equally important friends.

We Are Not In Competition With One Another.

Affirmation

See *DON'T COMPETE, Section 3, p. 214.*

References

Chapter 32

HOLD HOUSEHOLD COUNCILS

Gabriel was 14, bright and uncontrollably disruptive. When it came to rebellion, he was in the fast lane. His parents had required him to come and see me in order for me to "try and knock some sense into him."

Not wanting to be in my presence, which he saw as further punishment, he was smart-mouthed and swore to shock me. I learned of this only later because once he quieted down and softened up a bit (which took three or four visits), he said his original strategy was to swear in my presence because, inasmuch as I was a minister, he thought I would make him leave if he talked that way. When I didn't react to his language at all, it caught him off-guard.

My first few attempts at conversation were fruitless. He responded with as few words as he could, but with many grunts, "nope's" "yip's" and so forth.

In desperation I asked him to tell me his entire life story. "That's stupid," he declared, but launched in immediately. What I heard was a teenager who claimed that from the time he could remember he had been severely corrected and not allowed to talk freely. His opinions were denounced, his ideas declared unclear or unworkable. He felt as if he were under a waterfall of negativity and repression at the hands of his parents and he was "not going to allow them to get away with it."

His parents were happy when I suggested holding a weekly family council until I explained the guide-lines *(found in Section 3, p. 214)*.

They did not believe in allowing children to express ideas that were wrong, without making parental corrections. They saw making such corrections as being their responsibility. Furthermore, they were the parents, and to allow their children (they had three — the other two were younger and still cooperative) to speak their minds was a violation of the family structure they demanded.

I explained, as best I could, that I suspected that their son was in rebellion because he was "underheard." He felt like a bad, unwanted outsider. He felt squashed, unappreciated, and was striking out, attempting to join a family that didn't want him. "My parents want a robot, not a son," he once declared. I mentioned this and other things, including the fact that children and young people are often trying on ideas to see if they fit, just as they do with clothes. Even if they express their ideas by screaming, it doesn't always mean that they have adopted that position as a life-time philosophy. Also, children often will say things in order to shock their parents as a way of getting them to talk, or to punish their parents.

His parents left, feeling that I was taking their son's side, and they never sent him back to me again. I keep track of them from a distance and, from what I observe, the war continues; in my opinion, needlessly.

Comments The household council is an hour or so each week, or as often as is needed, when the family takes time out in order to get things straightened out. Everyone is allowed to speak freely. Listening, without correcting, criticizing, or violating the speakers' boundaries is necessary.

Food For Thought Do you conduct a household council?

❏ YES   ❏ NO

If not, are you willing to try it?

❏ YES   ❏ NO

One of the smartest things we've learned from strong couples is that, in some form or another, they have a household council, even if it goes by a different name.

A household council is a consistent meeting of all who live in the home.

Nearly always, my wife and I hold our household council in one of three locations: while on our morning walk, in the car, or in our hot tub. These locations offer us privacy and we are out of reach of radio, phone, TV, and the printed page. It is there that we feel most comfortable in placing all of our cards on the table, face up.

Comments

We Participate In A Scheduled Household Council.   *Affirmation*

See *HOLD HOUSEHOLD COUNCILS, Section 3, p. 214.*   *References*

95

Chapter 33
DATE 'TIL YOU DROP

D ates can be wonderful. Being on a date implies having fun and being away from obligations. It is a time to relax, to enjoy yourself with your partner, and to do something entertaining or recreational.

When we move into a permanent relationship, often the time, money, and energy formerly spent on dating soon goes toward bills and babies. Be that as it may, it is always a huge mistake to stop dating our partners.

If possible, recreate your first few dates. If for any reason that is not possible, find enjoyable things to do together.

Trade off each week the one who decides where to go and what to do.

If you have stopped dating, make the correction today. Plan at least one date with your partner each week for the rest of your life.

Our first dates were _____

_____

_____

_____

Now, I would like to go on the following dates

_____

_____

_____

_____

We Continue Dating One Another For The Rest Of Our Lives   *Affirmation*

Chapter 34

MAKE HISTORY TOGETHER

For both personal and professional reasons, I look into nearly everything published about relationships. As a result, an extremely useful insight occurred a couple of years ago.

My wife, Linda, and I spent several hours working with a psychologist charting our genograms. A genogram uses one's family-tree as a starting point. Genograms reveal repeated family traditions, habits, and patterns. The additional component is that it shows the kind, length, and quality of the relationships. That is, were they long or short, loving or violent, etc.

What I discovered was that the influential portion of my family had a repeating pattern: the men abandoned their families and the women responded by becoming fiercely independent.

What was startling about this revelation was that I had followed the pattern without consciously knowing it. I had abandoned my first wife and only son in lieu of my addiction to work. At the time, I loved and wanted to retain my addiction more than them. As a result, both of them became fiercely independent.

Can you identify the relationship and emotional patterns of your family?

Food For Thought

❏ YES ❏ NO

Are these patterns healthy or unhealthy? _____

A Suggestion No matter how you have answered, take the time to fill in a genogram. It will serve you well.

Imagine that your great-grandparents, your grandparents, your parents, and you are *Be sure and read your* sitting on a long, living room couch. *Family Scriptures!* Your great-grandparents are holding a book which has been handed down for centuries. This book contains your families' most treasured heirlooms. These heirlooms are not trinkets but the philosophical, religious, social, mental, and emotional foundations of your family.

That book is your Family Script in life. It contains all of the expectations and obligations, secrets, responses, habits — both good and bad — that they, and now you, are required to follow, if you are to be true and faithful members. Over the centuries, this Script has falsely become "The Family Scriptures." (Our true internal scriptures are found in the memory of our Soul — *see Chapter 9, Feed Your Soul.* Diversions such as activities and people, as well as the constant chatter of our mind, blinds us to their very existence.)

Your great-grandparents turn to your grandparents, pass the Family Scriptures to them, and say, "Now it's time for you to read this. Read it word for word. There are dire consequences if you change a single word." So, dutifully, your grandparents take the Family Scriptures and read them faithfully for their entire lifetime, only to pass them on to your parents, who in turn, take their turn reading and following the Family Scriptures. They then turn them over to you with warnings that you must follow, no matter what.

Affirmation We Know The Habitual And Emotional Habits Of One Another's Family & Culture.

References See *MAKE HISTORY TOGETHER, Section 3, p. 216.*

Chapter 35

ESTABLISH HEALTHY SYSTEMS

M aurice was tall and ugly. He was so strange looking that he constantly made jokes about his appearance. I suspected that he told jokes on himself in order to keep from hearing them. After getting to know him I realized that he was more comfortable with his looks than I had originally suspected. About his looks, he had a great sense of light-hearted, endearing humor. His sense of humor was a part of what had attracted Bernice, his wife, to him in the first place.

But all of that had grown old and they came to see me because Bernice had threatened to leave him. When I asked her why? she replied, "Because he's a &%$&@ pig." (I've left blank his country of origin but, if it's any comfort, they were both from the same culture.)

By that, she meant that he thought of himself as having received the divine right to rule over his wife and family as his father had ruled over his.

When asked, he said he felt he was right. By duplicating his father's attitudes and actions, he believed he was showing his father that he loved and respected him, and was being loyal to him and "his ways."

At this, Bernice expressed her real complaint. "Maurice is married to his father, not to me."

Maurice and Bernice were in more trouble than they knew or admitted to being. As children, they were raised in the country of their birth. When they came to this country, Maurice resisted the ideas clustered around equality of the sexes while Bernice embraced them.

For Maurice, it went even deeper than loyalty to his father. It was a part of his religion. He described himself as a fundamentalist. Bernice described him as a "rigid fundamentalist." His interpretation of his culture, family, religion, and holy scriptures were clear to him. There was a God-ordained hierarchy in all of life and it was to be obeyed even if it seemed unfair. "It isn't my fault that I was born a man," he declared.

Maurice believed that the proper hierarchy was God the Father, God the Son, God the Holy Spirit, human males, human females, human male children, human female children.

Bernice said that she had seen this coming from the moment she met Maurice but hoped that he would change, or at least modify, his stance. He refused because he saw his position as "standing for God's Truth."

What is the answer to this stalemate?

What I currently believe is that if partners are in agreement about the style of relationship they wish to have, it will work. In this case, Maurice should be married to a fundamentalist and Bernice should be married to a man who sees her as an equal. Or, perhaps more importantly, a man who sees her as equally important. If Maurice were able to do this, many of his positions would soften just enough to allow Bernice to continue in the relationship.

What happened? I encouraged them to seek the council of a clergyman of their own faith. When they did, the clergyman agreed with Maurice. Two years later, after many heart-wrenching put-downs, restrictions, and denunciations which included accusations of defying God, being unfaithful, and so forth, Bernice left.

In this story, are you Maurice or Bernice or the clergy or none of the above? _____   *Food For Thought*

How could this scenario have turned out differently?

_____

_____

_____

Is your form of relationship healthy?

❏ YES   ❏ NO

The relationship system we follow is probably a   *Comments*
revised duplication of the system our parents used.
Our relationship system is also influenced by our
personalities, our culture, and our religion.

The healthiest relationship systems are when both
partners truly agree with it, operate within its
boundaries, are genuinely happy, and are getting
their needs met.

We Practice A Relationship System That Is Healthy   *Affirmation*
For Everyone.

In *Section 3, p. 217* see *ESTABLISH HEALTHY SYSTEMS*.   *References*
Study this chart with your partner and negotiate any
changes that might be needed in your relationship
system.

Chapter 36

ADJUST TO YOUR MINI-MARRIAGES

When I got married the first time (I've been married twice and divorced once), I was not yet 24 years old. I had been raised in a very restrictive religious way (Christian, Pentecostal Fundamentalism) with harsh boundaries and rigid rules for doing and not doing everything. Of course, I carried my religious practices into my marriage.

We had gotten married with a number of mutually agreed-upon life goals.

But, life is not rigidly linear and is seldom predictable. Actual life-experience is reflective (allegorically speaking) of a court jester's throwing accidents, exceptions, U-turns, and newness into the pot while gleefully yelling "surprise."

My first wife and I never successfully adapted to the life-changing events that occurred as I graduated from seminary and we had our son. Nearly everything had changed and we had not adjusted to it.

All long marriages are made from a series of mini-marriages.

In retrospect, what I now see is that during the years we were married, we had dozens of mini-marriages. I knew nothing of this sort of thinking then. I thought that once an agreement was made, it was one's obligation to fulfill it — come what may.

Now I see that we must adjust to every mini-marriage.

Comments

Your initial period together (when you first started dating) was your first mini-marriage. The engagement period where one's focus is on the wedding day and honeymoon, is a mini-marriage. Once you were legally married, your former mini-marriages ended and the next one began.

Living without children, then having a child or two, and later as they leave one by one — each change is another mini-marriage. If your company was on strike for sixty-one days, that sixty-one days was a mini-marriage. Every significant change ends one marriage and starts another.

All human relationships, be they couples, triangles, foursomes, or whatever, including children and parents, cause diversion. Our lives change constantly and with each change our expectations and agreements must be revised.

Folks who demand that things stay the same are destined for unhappiness or divorce or both.

When change occurred, my first wife and I should have renegotiated everything — we renegotiated almost nothing.

Happily married couples are more like supple trees than cement walls.

I'll give an example of renegotiating. Perhaps, during a first mini-marriage or two, the wife agreed to pay the bills and keep the family checkbook up-to-date. But when the baby arrived, she was not able to continue. During that time, the husband needed to play that role. Perhaps years later, when the children were grown and out of the home, she would return to handling the bills.

In every case, flexibility is the key.

Food For Thought

So far our mini-marriages have been:

1. _____
2. _____
3. _____
4. _____
5. _____
6. _____
7. _____
8. _____

Affirmation

We Keep Adjusting To The Many Mini-marriages Within Our Greater Marriage.

Chapter 37

TAKE ONE ANOTHER'S TEMPERATURE

I came across the following while reading an interview with Marlo Thomas about her marriage to Phil Donahue: "We take each other's emotional temperature all the time. When one of us has to face a bad moment, the other is right there. No stiff upper lip in our house. We say right out, 'This is killing me...I can't stand this pain.' We expect to comfort each other..." (*Good Housekeeping*, April 1993, p. 190)

Here are some sample statements to get the ball rolling in your household.

- "You look worried, what's wrong?"
- "Is this a good time to tell you how I feel about my conversation with so and so?"
- "That phone call seemed to trouble you."
- "I have an idea. Let's take a walk."
- "Did that bother you as much as it did me?"
- "I wouldn't like that if it happened to me."
- "How did you feel about what he/she said?"
- "What bothered me about that was..."

Comment

In most offices, stores, restaurants, and cars we have both furnaces and air-conditioners. We adjust the temperature to meet our needs so we are comfortable — not terribly hot or miserably cold. Should we not treat ourselves as well in the emotional environments in which we live?

Another part of this is to take our own emotional temperature. A good way to begin is to ask ourselves during our internal self-talk, "How do I feel at this moment?"

Food For　I would like my partner to take my emotional
Thought　temperature by asking or saying things like:

_____

_____

_____

_____

_____

Affirmation　We Are Always Taking One Another's Emotional
Temperature.

Chapter 38

PREPARE FOR LOVE-MAKING

O ne of the reasons Max and Jane came to see me was that their love-life had ceased to exist. Jane said that her mother had warned her that regular sex would happen only for a few years after they married. Jane was convinced that this "pearl of wisdom" was wrong, and that it was her mother's way of reporting what had happened to her.

Whether true or not — actual fact or old wives' tale — the problem was that Jane was experiencing it and it terrified her because, among other things, she was afraid of "losing my husband."

Intimate love-making is always sensual but not always sexual.

It turned out that that wasn't an immediate problem because Max had lost all interest as well. They were now more like semi-compatible friends generally sharing similar lives. Their relationship was more like a contractual partnership than anything resembling an intimate marriage.

Max said, "I no longer have any zip." Jane said, "I'm more interested in other things and seldom think about sex." Yet, both identified sex as the major missing ingredient in their relationship. It wasn't. What was missing was intimacy.

Max and Jane had been raised in similar environments. Their parents maintained an emotional distance, not only from their children but from relatives, friends, and each other. Even though they loved one another, were faithful (as far as Max and Jane knew), they seldom touched one another and they never saw their parents sitting together or holding hands, to say nothing about kissing.

When I began talking about intimacy rather than

sex as the missing ingredient in their relationship, both sat quietly, hardly moving. Later they said they had never heard of such a thing (to be sure, they had heard the word "intimacy" but never in the context I was pointing out).

Both had emotional wounds that were caused not by terror or violence but by lack of emotional contact. Their parents were good parents but, emotionally, they resembled frozen statues. Without knowing it, Max and Jane had copied their parents' patterns.

I gave them a copy of the following paragraphs and asked them to read them before our next meeting. They did. Before proceeding with their story, please read what I gave to them.

Current research has discovered that men and women want nearly identical things in a relationship.

We want our partners to be monogamous, supportive, and fair. With them, we want to experience freedom from worry and a sense of safety for the rest of our lives.

The heart of intimacy is sharing privacy.

We want partners who will not leave or run away, mentally, emotionally, or physically. Some people have the annoying habit of mentally checking out during a conversation. Others leave physically during difficult moments, or during dreadful and dangerous times. Leaving includes diverting our attention onto something or someone else; i.e., a game, newspaper or magazine, person, hobby, an activity, or drug.

There is a word that contains the essences of what the research has found we want; that word is "intimacy." Authentic intimacy includes sexual intimacy but far, far more.

We've all seen tropical fish swimming on display with strong lights behind them. During those moments, it is possible literally to see into them. We might see their bones, their heart beating, and a few other internal organs. Metaphorically speaking, intimacy is a combination of attitudes and actions that allow our partners to see into us. Intimacy is the experience of welcoming our partners into our private worlds, to know us nearly as thoroughly as we know ourselves.

One way some people initiate intimacy is by taking off their clothing. Allowing ourselves to be seen naked may be a prelude to authentic intimacy but it is not the real thing. Another prelude, or perhaps I should call it a pretender, is having sex. Sexual intercourse is often a counterfeit for intimacy.

Beyond nakedness and sex there is a more advanced step — making love. Making love and having sex look a lot alike but they are as different as is the inside of a refrigerator from the inside of an oven.

We can have sex alone while masturbating. We can have sex with a person or a device. But making love requires time and deep feelings, feelings such as liking, loving, caring, and respecting our partner.

Rather than nakedness first, sex second, and making love third, there is a far more reliable order. It is spending time together first, intimacy second, commitment third, followed by making love which may or may not include nakedness and sex.

Many women report that they would rather cuddle than climax.

When Max and Jane returned they came with a handful of questions. What they said was that they had been so frightened by reading these paragraphs that they hadn't talked about them at all.

Have you found yourself in this story? ❏ YES ❏ NO

Are you Max or Jane or one of their parents? _____

Food For Thought

Is it true that you are afraid to expose your inner self, even to the one you love?

❏ YES ❏ NO

Comments   We all know that it is not unusual for married couples to have a rather predictable, even boring, sex life. Familiarity breeds complacency, for as we all know well, the hundredth time we do anything, no matter what it is, it is less challenging or exciting than the first time.

In order to satisfy our partners, not only sexually but in all other ways, we need to ask them what they want and what they do not want and how they feel about each. Gift-giving, meal-preparation, and love-making have a number of things in common. Nothing is more important than knowing how our partners feel now and what they want now. This piece of information is worth its weight in gold.

Prepare for love-making with the same thoughtfulness you would use when preparing your partner's favorite meal.

Affirmation   We Prepare For Intimate Love-Making.

References   For more about Max and Jane, see *PREPARE FOR LOVE-MAKING, Section 3, p. 221.*

Chapter 39

Don't Blame

J ane started our first session with a startling
revelation. She and her husband, Malcolm, who
was seated next to her, had "never" gotten along. Her
announcement seemed an exaggeration, but he
nodded in agreement.

During our next few meetings I came to realize that
Jane was one of the most brilliant and articulate
women I had ever met. She graduated *magna cum
laud* from a major American university. According
to Malcolm, it was an honor which she made sure
everyone eventually knew. She didn't deny it; she
only looked at him with a nasty face.

They had concluded that if they could somehow
magically solve their problems, they would end up
happily married. And, of course, they were right. But,
they had been looking in the wrong place for their
solutions.

At my urging they saw a sensitive and brilliant
psychiatrist with whom they worked for many
months. Eventually they unraveled the truth. They
returned to see me only once to thank me for the
referral and to tell me what they had learned.

Their real problem was two-fold. Malcolm not only
felt inferior to Jane but inferior to all people,
especially women. Jane not only felt superior to
Malcolm but superior to all people, especially men.

They were perfectly matched because one of the
functions that relationships perform (relationships in
general and intimate relationships in particular),
better than anything else, is to bring all of our
unfinished business into perfect focus. They each had
married one of the people on the planet who had all
of the built-in qualities to ignite their primary flaws.

Jane's endless disagreements with Malcolm were her way of waging war against a world which she secretly feared hated her because she was smart. She had placed her intellectual brilliance in front of her, both as a badge of honor to brag about as well as a shield to hold others at bay. It worked.

People always praised her for her ideas but no one — not her parents, friends, or Malcolm — really loved or trusted her. She was never asked to lunch or to social events unless they were required. Emotionally she was a dry sponge and she was desperately lonely.

In moments of anger, Malcolm would fly into a rage and call her "Comp," short for computer. His sarcastic explanation (which stemmed from his inability to break through his and Jane's defensive structures) was that "computers are wonderful for calculating but you wouldn't want to take one to bed."

Jane was equally caustic by generalizing his behaviors as mirroring the basic make-up of the entire male population.

They learned that they were both starved for love and acceptance and they were asking for it in the only way they knew. Behind the scenes, they were waging war with their own thoughts and feelings which they only imagined others were thinking and feeling.

Jane's conclusions that people didn't like her because they were jealous of her mental brilliance was a cover up for the truth. The truth is that when one brags about himself or herself and denounces the opinions of others as inferior or wrong, it becomes a barrier. Bragging is a way of placing ourselves on a higher pedestal than others. It is difficult for most folks to warm up to a braggart.

Jane's real war was with her inner critic, an internal voice that relentlessly pushed her to achieve in order to prove to herself that she was worthy of being liked and welcomed into others' worlds. It hadn't worked and never would.

Malcolm's war was with underachievement. His internal critic was so severe with him that he questioned everything he thought, felt, said, or did.

According to him, during his entire life the one and only person he ever stood up to was Jane. Somewhere along the line, probably early in his childhood, he concluded that the best way to be liked was to never outdo anyone. By "not winning" and not beating anyone at anything, he would be liked. They would like him because he would always appear to be inferior to them. Feeling that he was inferior would then translate into their feeling no competition from him, and he would be allowed into their circle. This strategy worked reasonably well.

Jane had down pat "how to influence people." The part she was missing was "how to win friends." By the time they returned to see me, she was well along the line in breaking her habit of bragging and denouncing the ideas and opinions of other, including those of Malcolm.

Malcolm was having more difficulty recovering than Jane. His internal critic (which rendered him as one who was demon-possessed) was still in charge of his thoughts and feelings. Whenever he stood up for himself during the day or expressed an independent opinion, he would spend a restless night reviewing the "encounter" and dreading the consequences. There were seldom any consequences because others were glad to hear his opinions. But, he fantasized that they would render him an outcast. The fact that no one ostracized him was difficult to trust because he further believed that they were now just putting up with him and being falsely nice.

Needless to say, with all of the above out in the open, their relationship improved. While with one another, they were "learning to hold our tongues" — she, in letting him (and others) speak without denouncing; he, by drumming up the courage to say his truth in a non-sarcastic manner.

Food For
Thought

Do you identify with either Jane or Malcolm?

❏ YES ❏ NO

Are you acting outwardly in a false manner in order to lord it over others? ❏ YES ❏ NO

Are you acting outwardly in a false manner in order to be liked by others? ❏ YES ❏ NO

What do you need to do now? _____

_____

_____

Comments Some people have become accustomed to blaming their problems for their inability to get along. Years of research have uncovered this: problems themselves are not the problem. Married couples, the world over, face nearly identical problems. For example, rich folks often fight over money more than poor folks. All healthy individuals, relationships, families, households, friends, and business colleagues have conflicts and problems. It is how the problems are handled that is critical.

Affirmation We Don't Blame Our Problems For Our Problems.

References See *DON'T BLAME, Section 3, p. 228.*

Chapter 40

DON'T PUNISH ONE ANOTHER

Crystal and her husband John came to see me. John had demanded the meeting because his wife was running his life and the house "like a Nazi concentration camp."

What broke the camel's back was their son, Ed, telling her that he had cleaned his room when he had not. For that lie, Crystal sent Ed to bed without supper. In the morning, after her husband had gone to work, she locked him in his room all day and let him out just before John returned from work. She warned Ed and his two sisters to keep quiet about it. However, one of them told their father. John felt that the punishment was excessive and that his wife was out of control, and I agreed with him.

Crystal explained that she had been raised in a strict, religious household where rules were followed without exception. As she remembered it, this did not bother her until she was a teenager. During her teen years, she spent a lot of time thinking of ways she could be a normal teenager without breaking the rules. She still felt the rules were essentially correct even though she felt compelled to resist them.

When she got married and had children she found herself becoming angry and, she admitted, unreasonably punitive whenever her children or her husband violated a rule. She found herself less occupied with correcting the violations than punishing the violators, and doing so severely.

During a series of conversations we had on all manner of subjects, Crystal came to realize that her need for rigidly obeying rules and dealing out cruel punishments had their genesis in her childhood home and religion. She was taught that this was the way God was and we should follow His example on earth.

She recognized that her preoccupation with punishment was "crazy," yet she was also afraid of the consequences of "letting go." She wanted to loosen up a bit but didn't know how, and she was afraid that God would retaliate against her if she did.

I frequently recommend books to those I think will read them, and I encouraged Crystal to purchase *A Course In Miracles*, published by the Inner Peace Foundation, and another book called *Creation Centered Spirituality*, by a then-Catholic Priest, Father Matthew Fox. Both books encourage the reader to relinquish the need to give and receive punishment, a need bequeathed us by our religious traditions for the correction and expiation of sin.

For Crystal, struggling with this need has become a life-long fight. Currently, she is caught between believing that this approach is good and fearing it will undo her. She retains a huge amount of fear. She feels guilty and afraid of "not doing God's will" when she corrects rather than punishes.

As I mentioned in the prologue, the suggestions in this book do not provide a quick-fix. Until she realizes that the idea of a vengeful God is one of the most insane ideas humans have ever invented, Crystal will continue to struggle. Hopefully, one day she will give up the idea of a vengeful God in favor of a thoughtful, loving God. Meanwhile, she is attempting not to punish her partner and her children for what she perceives as their mistakes.

Food For Thought   Do you identify with someone in this story?

❏ YES   ❏ NO

If you do, which person are you? _____

Do you ever punish your partner?

❏ YES   ❏ NO

Sometimes, do you delight when your partner gets hurt?

❏ YES   ❏ NO

Comments

Speaking with an evolutionary timetable in mind, civilization is still in a relatively primitive state. We are still punishing wrongdoers rather than helping them correct their mistakes. Just as there are people with physical diseases so developed that modern medicine can do nothing but send them home to die, so too are there people who are so psychologically wounded that, for our protection, they must be locked up. Hopefully, the day will come when we will be able to bring healing even to serial killers.

In the meantime, education and correction must begin replacing retribution and punishment. I do not mean to imply that we should free all prisoners, for, as I've just said, some people are so mentally, emotionally, and socially ill, and so spiritually depleted, that they are beyond even our most advanced healing practices.

However, healthy partners are ahead of society in this regard. Just as algae grows naturally in stagnant water, so errors (or mistakes, sins, thoughtless and evil deeds) grow naturally from internal wounds. Sometimes our "internal wound" is nothing more than the lack of correct information. Sometimes it is produced by abuse.

Healthy partners seldom punish one another. More often, they cluster in order to find a better way, and to make healthier choices the next time.

Affirmation

I Do Not Punish My Partner For Mistakes.

Chapter 41

DON'T SLAM ONE ANOTHER

For nearly a decade, Ed had a recurring dream. In the dream, he and his wife Anita are kneeling before a Confessional. His sin is that he has eaten chocolate cake for breakfast. As he begins his confession, Anita starts to berate and belittle him in front of the priest, calling him names and accusing him of disobeying his mother. Ed then pulls a butcher knife from under his coat and repeatedly stabs her until she is dead. Ed awakens, trembling.

Ed's dream was mirrored in everyday, waking life by a wife who criticized him incessantly. Anita's criticism was most pointed when Ed dared to stand up for himself by disobeying her. According to Ed, Anita did not like the way he dressed. She did not like his hair style, the color of his car, and so on. According to Ed, she didn't like anything about him at all. When I asked him what Anita would say about this, he said she would say he was exaggerating.

I suggested he tell her about the dream, along with our interpretation (he and I agreed on the meaning of the dream). For a few weeks, he refused. Then one night the dream recurred. He asked her to come in with him to see me.

When they arrived, I became aware that I was prejudiced against Anita, but I tried not to be influenced by this. I noticed how Anita corrected nearly everything Ed said, but I took care not to confront her with this observation. In essence, I verified everything that Ed had told me he experienced with her.

It was clear that Ed was frightened to tell his wife about his dream, and, as it turned out, for good reason. Ed began by telling Anita that he had a dream for ten years in which she figured. He then told her what I had taught him about recurring dreams. They are the equivalent of the subconscious part of our mind yelling loudly and insisting that we pay attention to something extremely important.

With great reluctance he told Anita the substance of the dream and added my guess about its meaning. Without saying a single word, Anita got up, walked out, and never returned.

Ed tells me that they have never spoken about the dream again. He reports that she has let up on him somewhat but that, in general, the pattern continues. He also reports that the dream has never recurred, which indicates to me that our interpretation was correct.

The conspiracy of silence that prevails in Ed and Anita's household keeps them together in a situation many other couples would find intolerable.

Food For Thought Do you criticize or denounce the things your partner enjoys?

❏ YES ❏ NO

Does your partner look down upon your interests?

❏ YES ❏ NO

Are you willing to sit with your partner and talk about how you feel when you are on the giving or receiving end of this kind of "put-down?"

❏ YES ❏ NO

If not, what are you afraid will happen if you do?

_____

Healthy individuals allow their partners to pursue their interests without denouncing them or threatening retaliation.

Whatever your partner's tastes in music, food, clothing, movies, movie stars, books, organizations, political ideologies and politicians, ideas, or opinions of every sort, you show you care by respecting your partner's choices, particularly when they are not the choices you would have made. While I happen to know some women who go to sporting events with one another, the average man likes sports more than does the average woman. I have never had a male friend call me for the purpose of our going shopping together.

Men who denounce women for getting together to talk or shop display a lack of social skill. This is as distasteful to women as it is for men to be denounced for playing or watching sports.

Allowing our partners to be themselves is a wonderful gift to give. Healthy partners do it all the time.

I Do Not Denounce My Partner's Tastes, Likes, Or Dislikes.   *Affirmation*

Chapter 42

MANAGE YOUR MONEY

The first time I met with Nash and Tracy (nearly twenty years ago) was during their pre-marital counseling session. The results of their personality profile showed that they were both compulsive. I asked them if they felt this was so. In unison they said, "Of course!" and they became instantly animated.

With gleeful delight, their faces now beaming, their bodies alive with joy, and their voices a higher pitch than before, they talked over one another in their enthusiasm for telling a difficult-to-believe tale.

Nash and Tracy had a lot going for them. They were young, healthy, well-educated, and both had high-paying jobs. Together, they had far more money to spend than they ever dreamed of having.

A few weeks earlier they spotted a new ski boat on an outdoor lot. Minutes later, they owned it. Before the day was over they also bought a boat trailer, a truck to pull them, and ski equipment. That afternoon, they spent more than $40,000.

"A happy marriage is the world's best bargain."

Tracy said she bought her wedding dress impulsively as well. I asked what it cost. Smiling she said, "Seven thousand."

Several months following their marriage, with their impulsiveness still raging out of control, they returned ready to face their addiction. I encouraged them to join Debtors Anonymous, which they did.

Six out of every ten reported household arguments are about money. Research has revealed that most of our money arguments are not directly about money. Money is the raw nerve, the easy-to-touch sore spot

Comments

that gets both the blame and the attention which rightly should be carried on the shoulders of other issues.

If money is your real problem, the solution is remarkably simple: assemble all parties involved and make a mutually agreeable, realistic budget and stick with it. That's it!

However, if all parties agree to arrange a meeting in order to set up a financial plan but no meeting takes place or, if a financial plan and budget is adopted but not adhered to, a Hidden Agenda is lurking nearby. Not dealing with our hidden agendas is similar to making the bed while knowing there are rattlesnakes under it.

Food For Thought

Do you identify with Nash or Tracy in any way?
_____

What have you done about it? _____

_____

_____

If spending and money are not the real reasons for conflict with your partner, what are the reasons?

_____

_____

_____

_____

What would your lifetime budget look like? _____

_____

_____

_____

Affirmation   We Keep Our Budget(s) Up To Date.

References   For more about Nash and Tracy see *MANAGE YOUR MONEY* in *Section 3, p. 228.*

Chapter 43

DANCE TOGETHER

When asked to place their activities in order of importance, successful couples place high on their list spending a lot of time together. Their relationship is the highest priority in their lives.

This was not true for me during my first marriage. I placed my wife and son well down on my list — it was a huge mistake. High on my list was accomplishment, advancement at work, and doing the work of God and Christ thoroughly and well. At the time, I did not realize that my spiritual goals should have been being a healthy family man.

Therefore, one of the explosives I placed into my first marriage, thereby blowing it apart, was that I was a dedicated, practicing work-a-holic. I abandoned my wife and son both mentally and emotionally, and, at times, physically. When I was home, I was too exhausted to be of much help because my thoughts were still "at church."

Quality time means being alone and present with one another in body, mind, and spirit. It means being a skilled, active listener.

We Spend A Lot Of Quality Time With One Another.   *Affirmation*

Chapter 44

PLAY FAIR

B lair claimed that his wife, Maud, was "@#!*& manipulative." He further claimed that she was out of control and things were so bad he was thinking about not coming home for a few days "just to scare her and show her that I'm really sick of &@$#*."

He claimed that, without notice, she continually changed the rules. I asked if she denied doing this. He said, "No." I asked for a few examples.

"We agreed to invite our parents to our place for Christmas but not for Thanksgiving. One day I walked into the kitchen and overheard her talking with a friend on the phone about how she resented having to have her parents come for Thanksgiving again this year. When she hung up I asked about it. She said that her mother had called and complained that they felt left out, so she invited them. When I asked her why she didn't call and talk with me first, she said that she couldn't hurt her mother's feelings. I said, 'How about my feelings?' She said, 'I know you understand.'"

I asked how he felt about that. "Like killing her," he responded.

I asked for another example. "We agreed to go to Bermuda for vacation. That meant I had to take on a couple of extra clients in order to pay for it. [Blair is a lawyer.] About a month before we were to leave, the tickets and hotel vouchers arrived by mail. I opened the envelope and they were for Hawaii not Bermuda. I was so angry I threw them in the trash. When Maud got home I confronted her immediately."

"What did she say?" I asked. She said that both Bermuda and Hawaii are similar and our friends,

Harry and Harriet, might be able to join us in Hawaii but not in Bermuda. So she changed the reservations.

By this time I didn't have to ask how he felt. But I did ask how he felt about spending a significant part of their vacation with Harry and Harriet. "That wouldn't be so bad if I had been asked," he replied.

Without ever having met Maud, I already disliked her. Before meeting with Maud alone, I called a professional therapist friend of mine. I wanted to hear her advice about how to handle my interview with Maud inasmuch as I already disliked her. She gave me a wonderful piece of advice. "For now, don't believe a word her husband said. Instead, pretend that you have misunderstood the scenario and go into the interview with as open a mind as possible." It was good advice which I was almost able to follow.

The interview with Maud went well. What surprised and disarmed me was that her recounting of events did not contradict Blair's version.

Maud's explanation was that, even though she knew she should check with Blair first, whenever someone asks her for something, she feels terrified to not give in to their request immediately. She trusts Blair and is accustomed to his anger and is less threatened by it than by disappointing others. "It is safer to stand up to Blair's anger than to stand up for myself with anyone else."

Maud was so forthcoming that my qualms about her nearly vanished. A week or so later, the three of us met in my office.

By the way Blair said hello I could tell he was still angry and was ready for a fight. Without being asked, he began. He recounted several incidents similar in pattern to the ones I had previously heard. I didn't ask if they were new or old. Maud sat quietly without much reaction. She had heard and felt all of this before.

Blair was about to launch into yet another example when I stopped him. Turning to Maud I said, "Have you told Blair why you do these things?" She shook her head "no." I then asked Blair to not respond to Maud until she was finished.

She began telling Blair her truth. As far as I could tell, she said it all. It included that she never tells anyone how she really feels, nor does she express her real opinion, that she lives two lives: one with him and another with the rest of the world; and that he was the only person in the world that she trusts. She said that even though his anger was terrible, it was safer than the alternatives.

Blair had a great deal of trouble believing that what she was saying was true. Being an attorney, he was accustomed to confrontation, standing up for others and himself, and felt she must be that way as well. "I can't believe that you're that weak," he said. He also had difficulty realizing that during their six-year marriage he hadn't discovered these things about her.

Yet, now a little softer in tone, he said, "I'm sorry if these things are true but you have to stop treating me like this or I'm getting out [getting a divorce]." It was obvious that Maud had never heard those words before.

Comments

This story points out two things that happen often in marriages. The first is that Maud was not playing fair with Blair. She was using him to hide behind, mistakenly believing that his tolerance for such behavior was unlimited.

Second, it shows that sometimes we live with a person we don't know thoroughly. Many people, some married, some not, live secret lives masked off even from their most trusted friend. It wasn't so much that Blair's and Maud's life together was a lie. It was more in the category of no intimacy.

In chapter 38, Prepare For Love-making, I've written about authentic intimacy. I refer you back to that chapter while, here, repeating but one sentence. "The heart of intimacy is sharing privacy."

Do to your partner only what you wish done to you.

131

Maud had never shared her privacy — her secret, hidden, personal world with Blair. He found himself married to a person far more wounded that he ever suspected.

Both Blair and Maud went into therapy separately. Weekly, Maud attends group therapy where it is safe for her to practice telling her truth truthfully. Blair is involved with a group of men who are working together to stop their verbal battering. "I'm now living two lives," Blair told me recently. "At work, I'm hell on wheels. At home, I'm trying to be as gentle with Maud as I can."

Food For Thought

Does your partner really know you?

❏ YES   ❏ NO

If not, what parts of Blair's and Maud's experience hits home with you?_____

_____

_____

Note: If you have secret terrors as Maud did, I believe that it is not wise or healthy to sit down and reveal them to your partner alone. First, visit a skilled listener. Then, if and when the time comes to reveal yourself, do so with that professional listener by your side.

Affirmation   We Play Fair.

References   See *PLAY FAIR, Section 3, p. 231.*

Chapter 45

FORGIVE OFTEN

W hen successful couples are asked to explain what they mean by "best, dearest, or closest friend," here are some of their answers:

"I trust her more than any other person on earth."

"He's the one person I can talk with easily."

"I can rely on her."

"When I tell my secrets, hopes and plans to her, she doesn't laugh."

"I would rather be with her than any other person."

"I am comfortable going anywhere with him."

"It is never a burden to be around her."

"She doesn't drain my energy."

"When we're together, I feel better."

"She is the first person I call when something happens."

"If possible, I would marry her again."

"I am going to spend the rest of my life with her."

If you find that the above sentences do not describe your relationship, now is the time to face the truth, tell the truth, and make the necessary changes. Your relationship may lack trust, affection, or intimacy and therefore be more of a strained friendship than a marriage. Or, perhaps, it has become more like a business partnership than an intimate relationship.

We Forgive Often. *Affirmation*

FORGIVE OFTEN, Section 3, p. 231. *References*

Chapter 46

MAKE MOMENTS TO REMEMBER

A number of years ago I was called by the owner of a mortuary to conduct a memorial service. I called the widow in order to invite myself to her place to discuss her wishes for the service. She said, "We can handle the arrangements over the phone, now!"

I knew there was no point in arguing so I reluctantly began asking questions. "What did your husband do? What were his hobbies and interests? What clubs or organizations did he belong to? Where had you traveled?" and so forth. She answered every question briefly, usually with a simple "He/we never did anything like that." Finally, in frustration she said, "He never did anything. He never went anywhere. He was not interested in anything."

I prepared my remarks, and when I arrived for the service I saw her for the first time; she looked like a movie star. She wore black, and throughout the entire service she sat as elegantly as a model. She also wore a faint hint of a smile on her face. To this day, I suspect she had something to do with his early demise. He was 46. It turned out that she had no visible grief. They had failed to make any positive history together.

This is just the opposite of many widows and widowers I've met under similar circumstances. Often they talk about trips and events, they show me pictures, weep openly, and wish their marriage had continued forever. They had taken the time to create history together.

We make history naturally by experiencing with our partner extreme highs and lows. We do so by participating in events at home, play, or away that are retained easily in our memories. These are the things we recall and talk about. Some of them eventually are seen as the major events of our lives.

What I'm writing about is not necessarily a trip to Paris or an around-the-world cruise. It can be a wonderful walk, going to a certain movie, dinner with friends, and celebrating the holidays in a way that is enjoyable rather than depressingly stressful.

Food For Thought What are the four most prominent memories you have with your partner?

1. _____

2. _____

3. _____

4. _____

Would you like to repeat those events?

❏ YES   ❏ NO

What are four things you wish you and your partner would do together?

1. _____

2. _____

3. _____

4. _____

Affirmation We Make History Together.

Chapter 47

HAVE FUN

Patterns discovered during research indicate that happily married couples enjoy doing things together. They don't force themselves to do things together; they like doing things together.

Sometimes, this is as simple as reading in the same room, watching TV, or listening to music. It can also be quasi-work such as gardening, working in the same area on different hobbies, painting, or anything; or developing a history of laughing with one another.

Discovering that you no longer like doing things with your partner is, of course, startling. However, it is not a sign that your marriage is over. It is yet another indication that something is wrong and needs to be fixed.

The couple who laughs together, stays together.

Laughing is one of the most powerful natural medicines available to us and is a wonderful relational glue. Laughter is so important for the health of our relationships that, if it is absent in yours, you should import it.

Laughter can be imported by watching funny TV, watching humorous videos, listening to the radio, reading the comics, etc. Don't live without laughter in your lives.

I can bring the healing effect of humor into my relationship by: _____

Food For Thought

_____

_____

We Take Time To Have Fun With One Another.

Affirmation

Anatomy of An Illness, Norman Cousins, Bantam Books, 1979.

References

Chapter 48

GRIEVE TOGETHER

I have conducted several hundred funerals. One of the saddest, because it was one of the most psychologically ill families I ever encountered, was for a 65-year-old man who had recently retired.

For many modern people, grieving has become a lost art.

Upon arriving at their home, I was greeted gruffly by the man's two adult sons. They informed me that their mother was delicate; therefore, I should make my visit brief. "Help her be strong!" they insisted. In militaristic fashion they escorted me to her room. The moment she saw me, she began to cry. Both of her sons told her to stop — which, with great effort, she soon did.

During my visit her sons acted like guard dogs. They constantly patrolled our conversation watching for emotion. It was clear that showing emotion (and any grief over the death of their father) was against the laws of this family.

They interrupted our conversation by imposing their wishes about the service onto their mother. More than a dozen times, they referred to their father as having been "a man's man." They did not want any music because "funeral music makes people cry." They also told me a couple of funny stories about the man, instructed me to repeat them and say nothing that "would make anyone feel badly."

Just before the service began, the boys came into the mortuary office where I was putting on my robe. They informed me that their mother was having trouble maintaining her composure and that I was to conduct the service as fast as I could. During the service, they sat with their mother between them, their arms draped over and around her — restricting her (which was exactly what they were doing emotionally). During the entire service, one of them kept pointing to his watch and made circles with his hand which I interpreted as a gesture encouraging me to end soon.

Following the service I returned to the home along with many of their friends. The two boys had continued their frantic patrolling following the funeral service, at the grave site, and now at home. As I was about to leave, their mother said to me, "I was strong during the service. I didn't want to make anyone uncomfortable." Her statement made me feel uncomfortable.

Comments   Here was a family who were terrified of their softer emotions. I'm sure these men would feel free to watch a football game and yell and scream. But, to show that the death of their father bothered them even slightly, was forbidden territory.

The problem is that somewhere within them, all emotions natural to humans over loss lie fermenting. It takes a great deal of energy to force such emotions down (out of sight). Not allowed to be unleashed, they are destined to boil up in stress and dis-ease and perhaps eventually, even into disease.

The skill of grieving is as necessary to learn as is the skill of eating. Don't live without this skill.

Almost everything we know we learned from someone else. Some people are skilled at grieving — others aren't.

Affirmation   We Grieve Together.

References   To learn the difference between skilled and unskilled grieving turn to *GRIEVE TOGETHER, Section 3, p. 233.*

Chapter 49

MONITOR YOURSELVES

To my amazement, Jeff, who had been married for 24 years claimed that he never saw his wife's decision to file for divorce coming. He claimed that, as far as he knew, all was well.

What happened?

At least two things. In speaking with his wife, Jennifer, by phone (because she refused to see me with or without him), she said that over the years she just gave up. She claimed that at first he would look at her when she spoke but the last few years he would just stare. Finally, everything faded including her motivation to communicate. The second reason she gave was, "He's married to his business and doesn't even know it." It was true.

Jeff was not dumb. Being dumb was not the reason he missed the signals that Jennifer had sent out indicating that things were wrong. He missed them because his attention was on other things; namely, his work. Later he told me, "When Jennifer stopped talking, I thought it was because everything was OK."

A simple question or two each week would have helped. Questions such as:

Food For Thought

"Jennifer, I think things are going well for us; do you?"

"Jennifer, do you think I'm not hearing you about something important?"

"Jennifer, are we spending enough time together?"

"Jennifer, am I avoiding you in any way?"

Have you taken the time to ask any of these questions?

❏ YES   ❏ NO

Comments   We have learned that if we can afford it, it is a wise practice to visit the dentist at least twice each year for cleaning and a check up. It is also wise to have a complete physical examination annually. Happy, healthy couples have similar practices regarding their relationship.

Using dental hygiene and maintenance as a metaphor: it is possible to have relational bad breath, relational placque, relational cavities, and the need for parts of our relationship to be pulled out and replaced.

Using physical care as a metaphor: it is possible to develop relational aches and pains, to have a relational cold or flu, to have relational diseases that, if uncared for, could result in relational-death.

Withholding the truth sets into motion a slow, nearly unnoticed, type of relational decay. It is the foundation of that old saying, "Marriages break down long before they break up."

Affirmation   We Continue To Monitor The Health Of Our Relationship.

References   See *MONITOR YOURSELVES, Section 3, p. 236.*

Chapter 50

DON'T BE LONE RANGERS

With no end in sight, the existence of Twelve Step programs and other non-professionally led, on-going discussion and support groups, has been growing for two decades. Their success rates have sky-rocketed.

Life is far more complicated than ever before. Our lives are filled with a staggering number of options and choices, and enough pluralism to make the head of a god spin.

Fortunately, we now know that networking with others who are attempting to reach a common goal — whether that goal is to control an addiction or sell a product — is both helpful and necessary. The day of the Lone Ranger has passed.

This is true with highly successful married couples as well.

If you wish to create and maintain healthier relationships, one of the most efficient and effective methods is to meet, on a regular basis, with other couples interested in the same things.

Starting and maintaining such a group is not difficult. If you are not involved in an ongoing group that meets for the purpose of creating and maintaining healthier relationships, and you wish to be, you will find several suggestions by turning to DON'T BE LONE RANGERS, Section 3, p. 239.

References

We Are Not Lone Rangers.

Affirmation

143

Section 3

REFERENCES: WORKSHEETS, TOOLS, CHARTS, BACKGROUNDS AND EXPLANATIONS

EMULATE SUCCESS

Notes from Chapter 1

I T GOES WITHOUT SAYING that all of us have both strengths and weaknesses; we are naturally good at some things but lack skill at others. Some people are extremely good at getting along with others. If we want to improve our skill at getting along with others there is no better place to begin than by listening to, watching, and emulating those who have healthy personal relationships that are happy, mutually supportive, and last a life-time. The following information are some of the things these people do to create and sustain healthy relationships; just as important: from them we also learn what not to do.

Would you list your parents or other relatives as examples worth emulating? How about any of our recent Presidents' having a relationship you would want to emulate — couples such as the Roosevelts, Trumans, Eisenhowers, Kennedys, Nixons, Fords, Reagans, Bushes, or Clintons? How about other famous couples?

I WISH TO EMULATE:

_____

_____

_____

_____

_____

SPEAK GENTLY

Notes from Chapter 2

I T HAS BEEN SAID, "The more we know and the earlier we know it, the better off we are." This is true with anger. Anger, like every form of pain, is a part of our early warning system. It alerts us when something is wrong; it is a call for our immediate attention. We may have just experienced a put-down, heard that our partner has been unfaithful, have been the recipient of a verbal blast, or any one of a thousand pain-causing experiences. Violence is a natural response to injustice; whether the injustice is factual or fantasy makes no difference.

> *Sometimes our anger has little or nothing to do with the other person. Instead, it is a loud call from within, meant to shock us into paying attention. It may be an internal voice screaming, "Help! Face your addiction now," or, "One of your internal wounds needs care — immediately."*

All of our emotions are good, none are bad. Our emotions get our attention. Emotions teach us; they make us aware of the degree of safety or lack of safety of a given situation.

Like any wounded animal who feels defensive and wants to be left alone, when we are hurt, we act protectively as well. Sometimes we act mean, sometimes vicious and deadly.

When persons are violent with family and friends, it is not a case of being evil; they are hurt in some way. Their wounds may have been open and sore for many years.

When we encounter such a person, what we often hear is "Get out of my way or I'll kill you." It is extremely difficult to look past such a vicious warning and hear the real message. What we seldom hear is, "I'm afraid and I'm suffering. I'm hurting and I'm seeking your help in stopping my pain."

The deep roots of violence can grow from several sources:

1. *Unresolved, privately felt and held, psychological issues. (The term "psychological needs," as I use it, includes mental,*

*emotional, and spiritual needs.) Often violence originates from
unmet infantile needs. As I wrote earlier, as infants, we need to be
fed, safe, warm, dry, clean, welcome, touched, stroked, played
with, and talked to. We need to receive assurance that we are an
accepted member of the group. Our infantile needs continue
until the day we die; therefore, a more accurate term is "human
needs."*

As infants, when our human needs are not satisfied, we react, usually by crying or in some fashion that resembles grabbing. It is normal for children who do not get their human needs met to conclude that something is wrong with them.

We speculate that they perceive their needs not being met as punishment for having done something wrong (maybe something as simple as being born and intruding on their parents). Some get the idea that they do not deserve to have their needs met.

As an infant grows into a child, in a desperate attempt to satisfy these needs, he/she may begin to act in attention-getting ways, ranging from crying, sulking, and silence, to yelling, being destructive, becoming a prankster, a pest, or an aggressive bully.

The experience of lack and the fear of its continuing or recurring are huge in us (fear that there won't be enough food, safety, time, attention, or love). Unbridled selfishness, which is often denounced as sinful or evil, is instead the direct result of experiencing fear or lack. Even before knowing words, a child might feel and conclude that "I better get all I can because this may be all there is."

Like any hurting animal, we seem to be mean or selfish, but we are really afraid and hurting. We are calling out for our needs to be met in the only way we know.

The deep roots of violence can also grow from:

2. *Mimicking our ancestors, immediate family, extended family,
   community, and cultural patterns.*

We learn to behave more by watching others than by what we are told — actions teach louder than words.

If violence is a family tradition, the youngster learns violence. Eventually, it is deemed as an acceptable way of getting one's way. Children mimic attitudes, emotions, thinking patterns and thoughts, words, tone of voice, and actions.

149

The reaction to unmet needs can be expressed inwardly or outwardly. When directed outwardly, it manifests as hostility, rage, cheating, isolation, timidity, and the like. When directed inwardly it is experienced as fear which breeds addictions, uncertainty, despair, frustration, and anger.

My contributions to the collapse of my first marriage was my placing two explosives into it. The first explosive was being a work-a-holic and the second, being verbally abusive.

My habit of verbal violence began, innocently (in my mind), during grade school, by my teasing the girls I liked but was too shy to talk with directly. Later, as a way of covering up my interest in or affection for others, I extended this habit to nearly everyone. I became a "poor man's Don Rickles."

When verbal violence occurs in comedy skits, sit-coms, or in the theater, it can be extremely funny. Just as there are harmless secrets, so there are appropriate times and places where teasing is harmless. When done with great care, it can even be endearing. However, even when done in the theater, it must be done with some level of caution. And, when done among friends, there is a thin line between what is fun-making and what is hurtful; great sensitivity is required.

When we carry teasing into our marriage, as I did, we're playing with fire. For me, when it was fueled by anger or alcohol or both, it became a lethal weapon.

What I have come to know is this. Verbal violence was unlike the other explosive (being a work-a-holic) which I brought into my first marriage.

Verbal violence is a bad habit that must be replaced by a good habit.

Work-a-holic behavior is an addiction whose roots run deep within the history of my initiating families. Bad habits are relatively easy to overcome; addictions are difficult to overcome. It takes a life-long commitment to self-discipline and constant attention to one's emotions, thoughts, and urges to overcome an addiction.

Few relationships are killed instantly. Usually, they suffer long, slow, pain-filled deaths. Violence usually grows slowly but as it gains momentum, frequency, and intensity, it becomes a killer.

Verbal violence weighs in as the all-time heavy weight champion of relationship killers.

A Partial List of Violence & Controlling Behaviors

Excerpts from "Man Alive"

"...control works by physically, verbally or emotionally destroying your partner's physical and emotional integrity so that he/she will be afraid to be himself/herself, will control himself/herself, and therefore be available to be controlled by you."
— *From Man Alive (415/457-6760)*

Verbal Violence

Diminishing My Partner:
1. Belittling my partner
2. Mimicking my partner; e.g., imitating his/her tone of voice when he/she is angry
3. Patronizing
4. Being sarcastic to my partner
5. Criticizing/correcting/scolding
6. Responding to her/his concerns by instructing my partner
7. Insulting my partner
8. Ignoring
9. Being silent
10. Making sounds
11. Lying
12. Cheating
13. Name-calling
14. Rolling eyes

THREATENING MY PARTNER WITH WORDS:

1. Swearing and cursing at my partner
2 Shouting and screaming at my partner
3. Threatening the pet(s)
4. Threatening to throw something
5. Threatening to hit something
6. Threatening to have an affair
7. Threatening to prohibit my partner's social contact

EMOTIONAL VIOLENCE

Controlling My Partner's Time:
1. Usually being late or early for appointments
2. Vague about setting an appointment time
3. Not showing up for appointments
4. Delaying departures by loitering, fussing, or doing something else
5 Monopolizing the conversation

Controlling My Partner's Space:
1. Monopolizing shared space; e.g., playing loud music when my partner is reading
2. Invading my partner's quiet time; e.g., talking to her when she wants to be alone
3. Disregarding my partner's privacy; e.g., opening his mail
4. Ignoring boundaries; e.g., being affectionate when he said "no!"
5. Interrupting his sentences or activities
6. Last-wording; i.e., always having to have the last word in a discussion or argument
7. Interrupting my partner's sleep

Controlling Resources:
1. Withholding information from my partner
2. Withholding financial information from my partner
3. Withholding paychecks or other money
4. Monopolizing the checkbook
5. Monopolizing the TV or other household equipment
6. Withholding child care/visitations; e.g., last minute pickup cancellations
7. Having an affair

Using My Self to Control My Partner:
1. Sulking
2. Refusing to talk
3. Blocking efforts to mediate
4. Blocking efforts to negotiate
5. Strutting and posturing
6. Stomping out
7. Walking away
8. Hitting something

Controlling My Partner By Assigning Responsibility (Blaming):
1. Blaming something else for what you do
2. Blaming something else for what you feel
3. Blaming someone else for what you do
4. Blaming someone else for what you feel

Controlling My Partner By Assigning Status (Judging):
1. Putting people down
2. Categorizing; e.g., "Women are all the same"
3. Characterizing; e.g., "You're just like my father!"

PHYSICAL VIOLENCE

Physical Violence Around My Partner:
1. Throwing things close to my partner
2. Destroying things
3. Tearing out the phone

153

Physical Violence To My Partner:
1. Carrying my partner
2. Grabbing my partner
3. Shoving my partner
4. Slapping my partner
5. Hitting my partner

NOTES

	CHART I
	COMMON BATTERING TENDENCIES AND RESPONSES
Those With High And Healthy Self-Esteem	People with high self-esteem and who are skilled at conflict-management, never put up with abuse — their own or from their partner.
This category describes me and my situation. ❏ YES ❏ NO	The first time they abuse, they stop it. The first time they receive abuse, as a condition of continuing the relationship, they demand that it be the last. If they abuse a second time, they question their readiness for a relationship. They usually seek professional counseling. If they are abused again, they demand that they and their partner seek professional help immediately. If their partner refuses, they immediately and permanently end the relationship. They proceed with professional counseling and, when appropriate, begin to seek a partner whose self-esteem and conflict-management skills match their own.

CHART II
COMMON BATTERING TENDENCIES AND RESPONSES

Those With Unhealthy Self-Esteem	People who question their own self-worth and who are unclear about conflict-management techniques are willing to put up with low to moderate levels of verbal, emotional, and even physical abuse.
This category describes me and my situation. ❏ YES ❏ NO	The first time they abuse, they excuse themselves.
	The first time they receive abuse, they immediately question only their own complicity. "I must have done something to deserve this!"
	When abuse continues they further justify it as being caused by being tired, hungry, drunk, or whatever.
	When abuse continues they berate themselves for putting up with it.
	They think about ending the relationship, but continue to put it off.

CHART III
COMMON BATTERING TENDENCIES AND RESPONSES

Those With Damaged Self-Esteem	People with damaged self-esteem, and who are extremely unskilled at conflict-management, put up with all abusive behavior — that which comes to them and that which they dish out.
This category describes me and my situation. ❏ YES ❏ NO	The first time they abuse, they naively believe it will be the last time.
	Secretly, they believe their reaction was based on unusual circumstances or their partner is entirely responsible. *(Continued on pg. 158)*

	Chart III — *Continued from pg. 157*
Those With Damaged Self-Esteem	They say to themselves, "He/she deserved that. That will teach him/her (to watch out in the future, or teach them who is really in charge).
This category describes me and my situation. ❏ YES ❏ NO	The first time they receive abuse, they naively believe it will be the last time. Often they said to themselves, "I deserved that." "I will watch what I say/do from now on." When giving and receiving abuse continues, it convinces them that they are the sole culprit. The idea that both they and their partner are wounded, unskilled, and abusive never enters their mind. When administrating abuse, they see themselves as being justified because they are simply standing up to an abusive partner — fighting fire with fire. When receiving abuse, they see themselves as the cause, as permanently trapped, and unable to end the abuse. Ending the relationship may be terrifying because 1) severe abuse has been promised; 2) they have mistaken loyalty for love; 3) of family pressures; 4) of religious vows; 5) of ambivalence about living alone or having the full responsibility for the children; 6) financial uncertainty; or 7) because they tried leaving without professional help before and they were severely beaten upon their return. They and their partners continue to call the police, need emergency care, and continue to inflict damage on one another. Often these patterns continue for a life-time. It stops only when intervention is finally sought, or upon death — often by murder.

The first violent incident that I remember in my life occurred:

_____

_____

_____

_____

How does that incident effect you today? _____

_____

_____

_____

Complete this sentence: I am sometimes violent because _____

_____

_____

_____

As of this moment, what can you do to eliminate your violent feelings, words, or actions?_____

_____

_____

_____

If your marriage, family, or any relationship is to be healthy, violence cannot be tolerated. Violence, in any of its forms, is a killer.

Violence is justified only during the most extreme emergencies such as when saving a child during a life-threatening situation.

There is no way to over-emphasize the danger of killing your relationships when violence is present. My guess is that 80% to 90% of divorces are caused by violence of one sort or another.

If violence is in any of your relationships, know that it is a sick and deadly dance that must never occur again. Violence can be stopped, once it is admitted to, exposed, expressed, and help is sought.

Verbal violence is the most prevalent weapon couples use on one another. Couples who are skilled in relating with one another, seldom, if ever, batter one another. When they do, it is usually verbal battering only and they stop and make the correction immediately.

We, who are in the habit of using verbal violence with our partner, must learn to stop our conversation virtually in mid-sentence and immediately replace our old, sick, unskilled habit with a new, healthy, skilled statement.

ASSESSING BLAME

ACCURATELY ASSESSING BLAME for violence is difficult. It seldom helps and often exacerbates the situation, so why do it?

I am aware that there are many who believe and teach that men batter and women are innocent victims. My own study, as well as my experience as pastor, counselor, and a giver and receiver of battering language and emotional blackmailing, does not bear out this view.

Domestic violence is not a gender-specific problem, but it looks like it. Both men and women batter members of both sexes. The deep roots of domestic violence are embedded in patriarchal and matriarchal systems. Those systems were designed to protect from and control threatening or frightening people or situations. Patriarchal systems are often out front and easy to see. Matriarchal systems are the natural response to unfair patriarchal systems. Matriarchal systems are often more subtle and therefore difficult to see, yet are equally unfair and vicious.

Accurately assessing blame can become as endless as, "Which came first, the chicken or the egg?" A more accurate assessment is, "Domestic violence between adults is a two-way street and the cure must be, as well."

(See *Men, Women, and Aggression*, Anne Campbell, Basic Books, 1993; *Constructing the Sexual Crucible, An Integration of Sexual and Marital Therapy*, David Schnarch, Ph.D., W. W. Norton & Co. New York, NY, 1991; *Child Sexual Abuse: An Ecological Approach to Treating Victims & Perpetrators*, Drs. Noel Larson and James Maddock, W.W.Norton Publishers, New York, available early 1996.)

In the area of domestic violence, children are the only help-less victims. All others have options. When an adult, female or male, is identified as being the sole victim, that person may feel inept or justified in striking back.

Instead of focusing on blaming, we need to shift our focus to two people, equally wounded, unhealed, with internal mental and emotional wounds still open, who as children were victims.

Most often, wounds received from battering came from someone within their family or extended family. As adults, for good reasons they may be terrified, but they are not helpless. Skilled help is available in safe-houses, shelters, hot-lines, police departments, hospitals, and from professionals including doctors, nurses, social workers, attorneys, and clergy.

Blaming one person and exonerating the other distorts this issue. Such assessment is partially responsible for keeping the person who appears to be the victim feeling hopeless. Men are entirely responsible for their behaviors including their violence just as women are entirely responsible for theirs.

The confusion comes from two sources:

1. *As I said earlier, the part males play is easy to identify. The world over, we continue to live in patriarchal societies controlled by men where women are second class citizens.*

Dr. Thomas J. Brady, director of child and adolescent services in the McAuley Neuro-Psychiatric Institute at St. Mary's Hospital, San Francisco, stated it well. "The sociological side of this is that these men all grew up in a society where they were raised on

161

'The Rifleman' and 'Bat Masterson.' We were taught that the way you solve problems is through violence...When things go wrong, some turn to the childlike solution, and that's blowing people away."

"'Masculinity and self-esteem for some men mean performing and proving one's economic value; take that away and some men simply cannot deal with it,' said Mark Levy (a Mill Valley psychiatrist). Back in the '20s and '30s, men like this may have killed themselves, but now they turn their aggressiveness outward." - The *S.F. Chronicle*, 7-16-93, by Ramon G. McLeod.

"Many men still see women and children as chattel, and you can get an explosive situation when the woman decides to leave him," said Luanna Rodgers, a family therapist in San Francisco.

2. *Women, not men, show up in emergency rooms and seek shelter 98% of the time. In general, males are physically stronger than females. Men have a tendency to hit with fists, women have a tendency to hit with words. Males never arrive in the emergency room seeking aid for having been struck by a word.*

Women, fighting for their very lives, have created systems initially meant for defense and survival that have become more and more offensive.

Because men are usually larger, physically stronger, and often use their fists as weapons, they have taken the lion's share of the blame for domestic violence.

Women, because of their smaller physical size and strength, use other weapons. Often they revert to words that bite, bait, or batter. In moments when their very survival is at stake, they revert in desperation to primitive responses. They lash out as best they can. Sometimes they run and hide. Other times they withhold words or affection. They retaliate in any way available, including pushing, slapping, or throwing things.

When we are blocked, held down, not listened to, ignored, purposely misunderstood, or when, out of spite, our words are purposely misinterpreted, we do the natural thing; we lash out in primitive ways. During those moments, we are fighting for our lives as wildly and desperately as if we were being held under water by someone intent on drowning us. We are fighting instinctively with all of our strength because we are fighting from our primal instinct to survive.

162

What I believe now is that domestic violence, in all of its forms, is a destructive, two-way dance often participated in unconsciously by both men and women.

Often, our perception is that our partner is entirely responsible for its happening and we are entirely innocent. More accurately, violence is like the dance of addiction where one person is the abuser and the other person, unconsciously and unintentionally, supports the addiction. In domestic violence, this is what often takes place. For example, a couple has a wild and wonderful emotional beginning to their relationship. Some weeks later one becomes angry and strikes out verbally (verbally batters his partner). If the person who has been verbally battered has low self-esteem, he will put up with that verbal beating.

He may even blame himself for starting it and will begin the dance of "walking on eggs" in order to avoid setting off his partner. It is here, in the initial stages of the relationship, that the destructive patterns are allowed and established. If the recipient has poor conflict-management skills, these patterns will escalate. Escalation is when verbal violence leads to emotional violence and emotional violence leads to physical violence.

If, on the other hand, when the recipient has high self-esteem and is skilled at personal conflict-management in the home, he will halt the conversation and the relationship in their tracks. This person is so confident within himself that he is more willing to end the relationship than to put up with getting beaten. He also knows that whenever battering occurs, it must be addressed immediately. He may say something like this:

"What you just said to me is inappropriate. We cannot have a relationship if you are going to verbally batter me. I am not willing to continue this relationship like this. You have to express your anger, disappointment, and disapproval in other ways."

Everyone is capable of changing his verbal and physical habits.

SELF-ESTEEM

My True and Often Secret Opinion of Myself

The lack of healthy self-esteem (my true and often secret opinion of myself) is the root-problem with people on both sides of battering. Later we will see that one of the skills practiced by those who have healthy relationships is that they address their injuries. They seek help with the difficulty of feeling, identifying, and admitting to their injury.

REMEMBER...If you must "walk on eggs" in your home or workplace, you are a participant in some level of controlling behavior.

ADDICTIVE RELATIONSHIPS

Usually, people stay in addictive relationships for more than one reason. Often it is a combination of things such as low self-esteem, following family and extended family patterns, financial considerations, need for security, the love that happens in between violent episodes, fear of being alone, not wanting to disappoint parents and others, religious vows, or the hope that things will change.

However, sometimes they are simply addicted to the other person — they can't stand to be together because arguing and fighting seems constant, but they can't stand it when they're apart either; i.e., they feel something akin to home-sickness, jealousy, fear that the other person will not return, will find someone new, or whatever.

No matter what causes addicted folks to be apart—- it might be to go to the store, to work, or to escape following a fight — when the other person is away, usually both are obsessed with getting the other person back. People in addictive relationships report that the feeling of relational-love-obsession is identical to the craving of drugs.

Things are much different for those with high self-esteem. They come to their relationships well equipped to take good care of themselves. Often, they were trained with healthy family (and extended family) patterns to follow. They keep their financial house in order. They meet their own security needs. They are unwilling to put up with violence in their lives no matter its source. They do not fear being alone. They live their own lives, not the lives of their parents or members of their religion. Instead of obsession, they take good care of themselves.

If you are violent, today is the day to face it and stop it. Remember:

- Violence never helps (except during extreme emergencies such as saving the life of a child).
- Violence makes relationships unsafe.
- Violence is the Number One killer of relationships in our world.

One of my friends, Donna Ahlstrand, has written about violent fathers.

"Fathers should be role models. Fathers should not frighten children. Fathers should not do stuff kids would get in trouble for doing. Men are supposed to be strong and in control. Men aren't supposed to act like children. Fathers aren't supposed to frighten children. Fathers don't hurt mothers or children. Fathers should not be selfish. Fathers should not scare children and make them cry. Fathers should be dressed around their daughters. Fathers should see and acknowledge their children. If a father scares a child, he should apologize. Fathers should care about and take care of children. Fathers should be available to their children."

FURTHER READING

And Their Children After Them, Dale Maharidge and Michael Williamson, 1990. Received the 1992 Pulitzer Prize.

Backlash: The Undeclared War Against American Women, Susan Faludi, Crown. Received the National Book Critic Circle Award.

Becoming Your Own Parent, The Solution for Adult Children of Alcoholic and Other Dysfunctional Families, Dennis Wholey, Bantam Books, New York, 1990. A collection of 14 essays.

Boundaries, Where You End and I Begin, Anne Katherine, MA., Parkside Publishing Corporation, 1991. "Good fences make good neighbors" — Robert Frost. "Boundaries bring order to our lives...Boundaries empower us to determine how we'll be treated by others...When our invisible boundaries are trespassed by the thoughtless or intrusive actions of others, it is called a boundary violation."

Child Sexual Abuse: An Ecological Approach to Treating Victims & Perpetrators, W.W.Norton Publishers, New York (available early 1996.)

I Stop My Physical Violence To My Partner, First Stage Class Manual, Marin Abused Women's Services, Mens Program, 415/457-6760, Crisis Hotline 415/924-1070

Men, Women, and Aggression, Anne Campbell, Basic Books, 1993. A major study of female and, by contrast, male aggression and violence. Extremely helpful in understanding the opposite sex. Also see Anne's book, *The Opposite Sex,* 1989.

We Can Work It Out: Making Sense of Marital Conflict, Clifford Notarius, Ph.D., & Howard Markman, Ph.D., G. P. Putnam's Sons, New York, 1993

REPAIR YOURSELF

Notes from Chapter 3

NOT WANTING TO GET the cart before the horse, we begin with the essential first step —the life-long journey of self-repair. When we enter a smelly kitchen we have at least three options:

1. We can turn around and leave.
2. We can temporarily cover-up the foul odor by spraying the place full of room deodorizer.
3. Or, we can take the garbage out.

Clearing away the rubble that hides comes first. Interior rubble is felt as fear. The law of clustering (or "birds of a feather flock together") is helpful here because our fears feed and flourish side by side and, at times, on one another. So, when we find one thing we fear, it is easy to identify others.

If you often become angry or violent, if you sulk, brood, or move away in silence, you have unfinished business to handle. You can learn every new behavior (proven relationship techniques), but your internal rage or sadness will sabotage all of your efforts. And, if you do not settle your internal war, your new behaviors will not be natural — you will be pretending because you are still seething within.

Self-repair is one of the most important ideas in this book. If, in the past, you have been a person who is having difficulty maintaining peaceful, loving relationships that last, and you are now ready to reverse that trend, you have come to the right place. Even so, these ideas may be easy to read and difficult to face.

Many of us come into our relationships battered, tattered, and dismayed from other relationships. We are dominated with fear, mistrust, and resentment. If we are to have healthy relationships, we must clean up the messes we hear, feel, sense, or see within ourselves.

We can actually *hear* our mess talking. We can do this easily when we sit quietly and take notes of what our minds are saying to themselves. Our minds may be waging war. We might hear such things as, "I hate him!"; "I'd like to kill her"; "I would love to do something that would get back at him"; "Why did she do that?"; "He is such a ..."
We can also *feel* our mess. We do so by noting, mentally or on paper, tension in our body that arises when we hear warring words spoken by our minds. We can *sense* our mess when we feel ourselves being painted within by adrenaline or sadness. We *experience* emotions ranging from rage to virtual hopelessness when we are being painted into a corner.

We *see* our mess when we create relationships in the image and likeness of our interior selves — which is always the case. A lonely loner is first a loner in her mind. A killer is frustrated, first, in his thinking, and only secondarily, in his acting. A person who cannot keep relationships is a person who has not cleaned up his internal mess.

Speaking symbolically, self-scrubbing begins by stopping and taking a look into our minds. Our brain, heart, and guts are connected to virtually every cell of our body.

SELF-THERAPY OR PROFESSIONAL THERAPY?

I do not believe in Gestapo Therapies — those therapies that run rough-shod over people's defenses. I'll illustrate.

There are two ways to see into the center of a rose. We could tear one petal off at a time and eventually we can see the center. Or, we could nourish the entire flower by planting it in the perfect spot in rich soil, and water it properly. Eventually it will show us its center.

For two reasons, professional therapy is advantageous in our search for the things we need to clean up.

First, when we pay money to a professional, we usually don't waste our time beating around the bush, because we want to get our money's worth.

Second, a professional listener knows the territory. Once we accurately and truthfully describe what's going on within, the therapists can usually provide us with maps. These maps are worth their weight in gold, because they will keep us focused on staying on the main road and not diverting our attention to the side or back roads.

I am a great fan of professional therapy, and an even greater fan of trying to fix things alone first. Before going to a therapist, try cleaning up your act alone. Start here. The following are things I've heard people who have difficulty with relationships say they fear. Circle the things in the following list that you fear:

- rejection

- intimacy

- change

- talking

- sharing time

- sharing space

- sharing opinions

- sharing money

- sharing possessions

- being dumped

- not being attractive enough

- growing old alone

- being lonely

- not being smart enough

- not wanting to live with another mother-like person

- having to clean up my act
- letting someone know what I'm really like
- being confronted
- having to make commitments and agreements
- being sexual
- not being autonomous
- not being able to get out of a relationship
- being dominated
- not pleasing my parents
- not being in complete control
- repeating my past
- repeating past problems
- repeating my parents' marriage
- having my addictions exposed
- losing my freedom
- having to compromise
- not having my way all the time
- having my privacy invaded
- having to live in a way that is uncomfortable for me
- doing what I've seen done in other marriages
- having to change my habits

		THE QUESTIONS
YES	NO	
❑	❑	Do I have any addictions?
❑	❑	Do I have habits that cause others to distance themselves from me?
❑	❑	Am I lonely?
❑	❑	Do I lose my temper, or am I tempted to lose my temper, several times a day?
❑	❑	Do I have genuine peace of mind?
❑	❑	Am I truly happy?
❑	❑	Do I isolate myself?
❑	❑	Is it frightening for me to think about being alone?
❑	❑	Am I so opinionated and domineering that few people are willing to put up with me?
❑	❑	Do I enjoy and am I comfortable being intimate with another human? (This question does not refer to sexual intimacy. It refers to verbal and emotional exchanges that are honest and respectful.)
❑	❑	Should I seek help?

In trying to uncover the truth, answering the questions in the chart above has also been helpful to many. One caution about evaluating your answers: If you are lonely, and have difficulty in making and keeping friends, those facts are more telling than whatever answers you may have just given. Use every bit of courage you can muster and admit once and for all that you are not presently highly skilled at taking care of yourself. Remember, today is the day to begin because this affirmation is correct, *I alone am responsible for all of my attitudes and behaviors.*

We "scrub" our fears by talking to them as if they are a real person. I know this sounds crazy, but it's extremely useful. Because I enjoy the writing process, I would pick out the one that I fear the most and write to it.

Another step when doing self-therapy is reading about the specific fear you have uncovered. Look through the index of those books and zero in on your particular fear.

If you cannot find references to your fear(s), ask the librarian for help. Once you have accurate information, you can see if the lack of information is your problem; for many, it is. Then, act out your newly acquired information and see how it works. If you are still unsuccessful, it's time to find a therapist.

TALK RESPECTFULLY

Notes from Chapter 4

I F YOU FIND YOURSELF talking disrespectfully about your partner to others, it is a certain indication of trouble. Perhaps you are frustrated and afraid that the problems between you are impossible to settle. Your feelings of hopelessness are so overwhelming that you ridicule or criticize your partner to others.

One way to get clearer about the truth of your situation is to write affirmations. An affirmation is a statement that says it the way you want it to be. One of the most beautiful things about affirmations is that, after repeating them several times over a period of days or weeks, you will get extremely clear about what is true and, just as important, whether you really want things to change or not.

SAMPLE AFFIRMATIONS

I am married to my closest friend. Our marriage is healthy and strong. My wife/husband and I love spending time together. We are living life as God intends for us to live. We are mutually loving, supportive, and helpful. We have a great deal of fun together. We are one another's best friend. We respect one another. If given the chance, I would marry him/her again.

MASTER CONFLICT CONTROL

Notes from Chapter 5

ONE OF THE UNIQUE THINGS I teach is the difference between being assertive and being aggressive. Many people in our culture have these confused.

Some people who call themselves "strong" have aggressiveness and assertiveness combined or confused.

Perhaps they have been taught, by example and words, that aggressiveness means being strong and assertiveness means being weak.

Assertiveness always comes first. Aggressiveness is a last resort after all negotiation and reason has been exhausted. Aggressiveness is a form of violence: it is to be used *only* during extreme emergencies.

Culturally, we need to shift our thinking and our acting by realizing that being assertive includes thoughtfulness, using age-old manners, giving respect, and acting with equal care for ourselves and others. In the long run, being aggressive kills relationships while being assertive heals and enhances relationships.

In addition to accurate information and psychological health, everyone needs good relationships tools. Good tools make work easier. People caught in the destructive habits (in this case arguing and fighting) need tools that will help them to change their behavior more easily. The following worksheets have proven to be effective tools.

The next time you need to discuss an important subject, especially if that subject has been discussed before and now comes up again, before you begin, take the time to fill in THE SPEAKER'S PAGE and ask your partner to fill in their SPEAKER'S PAGE as well. When you come to the discussion prepared, your chances of reaching a successful solution soar.

INSTRUCTIONS FOR USING THE FOLLOWING WORKSHEETS

1. Agree on a subject. At the top of The SPEAKER'S PAGE complete the following sentence:

   The subject we have agreed to discuss is _____

   _____

2. While working separately, both you and your partner should fill in the answers in all five categories. Do this on your own SPEAKER'S PAGE.

3. In the columns following "I feel..." circle all the words which express how *you feel right now* while discussing this subject.

4. Before proceeding, answer the four questions.

   NOTE: When reporting your feelings...only report two or three at a time. When reporting "What I want." "What I don't want." etc., report one sentence at a time. Never overwhelm your partner with too much information at once.

5. As you listen to your partner reporting his/her *feelings* — on your LISTENER'S PAGE draw a circle around the words he/she report.

6. When your partner reports what he/she has written on his/her SPEAKER'S PAGE, you should record his/her answers on your LISTENER'S PAGE.

7. As skillfully as you can, discuss your findings.

   You may wish to refer to Chapter 24 "Establish Rules" to see the techniques that skilled couples practice.

THE SPEAKER'S PAGE

The subject we have agreed to discuss is:

Answer the following questions <u>with yourself in mind</u>.
Circle how you feel right now about discussing this subject.

I feel...

afraid	angry	anxious	awful
bad	confused	crazy	dazed
delighted	disappointed	distrusted	distrustful
elated	empty	embarrassed	ecstatic
excited	exhausted	fateful	fearful
finished	frustrated	furious	good
grateful	great	happy	hopeful
hopeless	ideal	listless	lost
lousy	nearly perfect	nervous	not understood
panicked	resented	resentful	sad
satisfied	stuck	terrible	terrified
troubled	uncertain	unhappy	unimportant
unsafe	used	wasted	weary
wonderful	wronged		

What I want is

_____

_____

_____

_____

_____

_____

_____

_____

_____

What I don't want is

_____

_____

_____

_____

_____

_____

_____

_____

_____

What I'm willing to do is

_____

_____

_____

_____

_____

_____

_____

_____

_____

_____

_____

What I'm unwilling to do is

_____

_____

_____

_____

_____

_____

_____

_____

_____

_____

_____

THE LISTENER'S PAGE

The subject we have agreed to discuss is:

_____

Fill in this page <u>while your partner reports his/her answers to you</u>.
Circle how you feel right now about discussing this subject.

The way my partner feels about discussing this subject right now is…

afraid	angry	anxious	awful
bad	confused	crazy	dazed
delighted	disappointed	distrusted	distrustful
elated	empty	embarrassed	ecstatic
excited	exhausted	fateful	fearful
finished	frustrated	furious	good
grateful	great	happy	hopeful
hopeless	ideal	listless	lost
lousy	nearly perfect	nervous	not understood
panicked	resented	resentful	sad
satisfied	stuck	terrible	terrified
troubled	uncertain	unhappy	unimportant
unsafe	used	wasted	weary
wonderful	wronged		

What he/she wants is

_____

_____

_____

_____

_____

_____

_____

_____

_____

_____

What he/she doesn't want is

_____

_____

_____

_____

_____

_____

_____

_____

_____

What he/she is willing to do is

_____

_____

_____

_____

_____

_____

_____

_____

_____

_____

_____

What he/she is unwilling to do is

_____

_____

_____

_____

_____

_____

_____

_____

_____

_____

One of the purposes of the following chart is to allow those who come from arguing and fighting traditions — and who are still caught up in following those traditions — a close-up view of those who use discussion as their means of coming to mutually acceptable agreements.

What we need to learn is to channel the energy generated by fear and anger into constructive paths; i.e., into mimicking the techniques of those skilled at conflict-management.

As you review the chart, "The Three Most Common Methods Of Conflict-management Used In The Home," give special attention to these three concepts:

1. Discussing gives birth to more discussing.

   Those who discuss were, in most cases, raised by parents (or under the influence of an extended family, community, or culture) who practiced discussing.

2. Arguing gives birth to more arguing.

   Those who argue were, in most cases, raised by parents (or under the influence of an extended family, community, or culture) who practiced arguing. They argue because they were never taught how to negotiate with someone they love or live with. These people talk and communicate but they talk past one another. They miss what their partner is meaning. They are not hearing the message that lies behind the words. Often, they think that arguing is negotiating.

3. Fighting gives birth to more fighting.

   Those who fight were, in most cases, raised by parents (or under the influence of an extended family, community, or culture) who fought. Watching and listening to adults fight, injured them emotionally because their "nest" or "world" was unsafe. Often, they think that fighting is negotiating.

The difference between those who argue and those who fight is more than style: it is a reflection of their own internal injuries and the severity of pain they cause when striking outwardly.

THE THREE MOST COMMON METHODS OF CONFLICT-MANAGEMENT USED IN THE HOME		
Discussing	*Arguing*	*Fighting*
People who are skilled at conflict-management discuss.	People unskilled at conflict-management argue.	People who have been emotionally injured fight.
They consider the other person a colleague.	They consider the other person a competitor.	They consider the other person an enemy.
The primary purpose of a discussion is to reach an agreement.	The primary purpose of arguing is to gain dominance.	The primary purpose of fighting is to damage the opponent and gain a victory.
Discussing gives birth to more discussing.	Arguing gives birth to more arguing.	Fighting gives birth to more fighting.
Discussing, arguing, and fighting reflect different levels of skill at conflict-management.		

Those who fight have been deeply injured, perhaps by something as simple as not having a positive example. In current jargon, they were raised in a dysfunctional family. They were taught that fighting was a permissible way to solve problems.

Let's pretend that you have been in an accident. You have several broken bones accompanied by lacerations and bruises all over your body. For weeks, whenever someone touches you on a black and blue spot, you flinch. At this stage of recovery, you are extremely touchy. People who fight have been injured. Emotionally, they are black and blue. Whenever one of their emotional black and blue spots is touched, they explode.

On the other hand, people who argue do not necessarily come from severely dysfunctional families. Their family and extended family simply may be unskilled when it comes to healthy negotiating in the home. Those who argue may simply be caught in poor habits.

DON'T ESCALATE

Notes from Chapter 7

HERE ARE FOUR THINGS TO DO:

1. Search within by listening to your brain talking to itself. Search to see if this conversation reminds you of former conversations that have caused you to become angry. You may be in need of dealing with your defensiveness, your short-fuse, and your ill temper with a professional. This hassle may have almost nothing to do with your partner.

2. Interrupt the conversation the moment escalation begins and rebond. Rebonding can take place by a nonsexual gesture or touch. This reassures our partner that we are allies and not enemies.

   Rebonding can also be done with words. "I know this is important for both of us, but let's not get carried away." "I don't want to argue with my best and dearest friend." "I'm your friend not your

enemy. Let's settle this in a way that will make both of us happy."
"Things will be better if we don't let ourselves get angry over this
discussion."

3. Choose your words carefully. Avoid shouting, swearing, and
blaming your partner for the way you feel.

4. Start your sentences with "I" rather than "You."

CARE FOR THAT INJURY

Notes from Chapter 8

SEXUAL MOLESTATION

WHEN SHE WAS A LITTLE GIRL, one of my friends was, periodically, sexually fondled by her father. She remembers that it
always started the same way. When alone together, her father sat
down next to her and placed his hand on her thigh. Slowly, he
massaged her thigh from side to side until his hand was rubbing her
between the legs. She put up with it as long as she had to but then,
too early in life, she had to set out on her own.

Falling in love prompted her to speak with me about this. She
reported — it was more like a report than a conversation — that
whenever her boyfriend placed his hand on her thigh, even if it was
in play, to show affection, or as a comforting pat that was entirely
nonsexual, she froze. The first few times this happened, her reaction
was so strong that he, feeling he had somehow hurt her, jerked his
hand away. In order to cover up her terror, she would smile at him,
assure him it was nothing, and take his hand and return it to her
thigh. Privately, she was terrified of her behavior, so mortified she
could not tell him why it happened. She came to me because she was
certain this wonderful man would leave her.

Several times I encouraged her to invite him to come to see
me with her. She finally did. The beginning of the session was
uncomfortable for all three of us. Later, he told me he was especially
uncomfortable because he never felt right when near a minister; also,
because she refused to reveal anything about the intended content of

our meeting. I was uncomfortable because I had no idea what would happen.

After the usual chit-chat, even though I knew the agenda, I asked what it was. He looked at her. She sat in silence staring at her hands. After a lengthy pause, she looked to me and whispered, "ya' 'ell 'em." I whispered back, "No, you need to say it out loud yourself." I assured her that she was in a safe place for such "telling." After another lengthy pause, she began, still speaking in a near whisper, completely unlike her usual robust, joyous self. She began telling her story, talking with uncertainty and not always audible or clear, in the way a shy child would talk. For those moments, her injured, interior-child was speaking. As she spoke, tears filled our eyes and, during her silence, we each sat weeping quietly as we shared pain.

She not only revealed the truth about anyone's touching her on the thigh, and her sheer terror that it would lead to abandonment by the dearest man she ever met; she also revealed several other places on her body which, when touched, would cause her to involuntarily recoil.

For anyone to be her partner, he would have to be extremely alert not to touch her inadvertently in a way that triggers memories of her father's molesting her. He would also have to be patient as the years quieted her reactions. Most of all, he would have to be someone who would not be crushed each time her recoil indicated a clear signal of rejection. He must be able to remember that she is rejecting her father's invasion, not her partner's casual touch. That takes a rare one — she's now married to him.

SOLUTIONS

STEP ONE in healing any emotional injury is awareness. As John Bradshaw is fond of saying, "If you can name it, you can tame it." If you remember your initial injury, you are fortunate.

If you are afraid of what you might find, do not explore your mind by yourself. Ask trusted friends and find a professional listener to walk with you in and through your memory. If you are not afraid, begin with some form of relaxation technique and allow your mind to remember by retracing every triggered event you can remember. Starting from the latest and going back to the earliest, relive the last event and allow the memory of what it reminds you of to flood your mind. Even as you remember it, you may, like me, hold a suspicion about yet an earlier one. Work with one memory at a time. After a half-hour or so accept your earliest memory as being the initial injury. If it isn't, you will remember an earlier one at a later time. If not, you're at target zero.

RETURNING TO THE SCENE OF THE CRIME...

By using our memory, we can walk backward in a linear line, moving from effect to cause and then from an earlier effect to yet another cause. The chain of cause and effect may be dozens of links long. Eventually, we come to the initial injury — the scene of the crime. Graphically, the process looks like the list on the next page.

If you are religious or spiritual, the lifting of guilt and shame can be aided or enhanced by prayer. If you are not religious or spiritual, or if you prayed and nothing happened, remind yourself over and over that you are injured, not because of anything you started but as the result of the emotional injuries suffered at the hands of your predator. I think that everyone who works alone up to this point should now find a reliable counselor to work with. The tendency to overlook something or to unconsciously hide from the entire truth is strong. Relax and seek help.

We name the initial injury by consciously noting the place, the circumstances, and the person or people involved. This remembering might include sounds, odors, fragrances, animals, the weather, or anything.

A Brief History of a Person Who Goes Nearly Out of Control Whenever His/Her Ideas are Challenged.

The initial occasion (scene of the crime)	Once, while at a restaurant, when I was 6 years old my mother embarrassed and humiliated me by calling me stupid.
Another incident	My second grade teacher criticized me in front of the class. I wanted to quit school.
Another incident	My closest friend told our secret out loud and everybody laughed. I didn't talk to him for several weeks.
Another incident	My boss said I made "a stupid decision." I wanted to hit him. I quit as soon as I found another job.
Another incident	I overheard my wife saying that I wasn't very bright. I refused to have sex with her for months. I never told her why.
The latest incident	While watching a sit-com, the father in the family was put-down by his entire family. I became furious but smiled along with every one else.

STEP TWO is remembering so many details that you cannot repress it again or dismiss it as a bad dream. This is done by some type of *reliving* the event as accurately as possible. If you like to write, write about it. Perhaps you could write it as a documentary, a poem, a metaphor, or as a novel about yourself or someone else. You may want to draw or paint the scene. You may want to re-enact it during professionally led group therapy where family sculpture and psychodrama are employed. Use whatever works for you.

STEP THREE is forgiving yourself. If you were an infant or child, there are still some things for which you need to forgive yourself. For example, in the case of being molested, forgive yourself: first, for not being God; second, for being too young to prevent it.

Some people report, with confusion and horror, that as the molestation reached its peak, they became aroused, stopped resisting, and, on occasion, achieved orgasm, only to feel at the same time utter shame and some responsibility.

STEP FOUR is forgiving the predator(s). Forgiveness does not mean approval. Forgiveness does not let the perpetrator off the hook.
The type of forgiveness I'm writing about is the type where the truth is brought out into the open. An intervening moment must occur. An intervening moment brings an immediate halt to the activity.

Usually an explanation either is or will be interpreted as an attempt to further cover up the crime. Nevertheless, a profound apology accompanied by financial help with therapy, if therapy was employed, should follow. Both parties should see a counselor together. With professional help, everything can be brought out into the open and new boundaries established.

In this regard, I highly recommend *Boundaries: Where You End and I Begin*, by Anne Katherine, M.A., Parkside Publishing Corp., 1991. After reading Anne's book, it will be clear when, how, and whom to tell and whom not to tell.

FEED YOUR SOUL

Notes from Chapter 9

RESTAURANTS THROUGHOUT the world serve food for the body. Some restaurants feature quick-service and "fast-food" while others encourage elegant dining with leisurely service. Our culture, family traditions, momentary mood, and financial circumstances determine which restaurant we choose.

Metaphorically, religions are restaurants; religious writings are the menus; and religious teachers are the waiters and waitresses.

We don't eat the restaurant (religion) or the menus (scriptures or religious writings) and certainly not the waiters or waitresses (religious teachers). We eat the food. Soul food comes in vast varieties. The energy created by spiritual nourishment propels us toward God, good, inspiration, and excellence, and creates clarity, comfort, hope, and enthusiasm.

Religions are institutions or movements designed to help people live psychologically healthy lives; i.e., to have mental, spiritual, relational and emotional health. Just as there are healthy and unhealthy people and businesses, so there are healthy and unhealthy religions.

Healthy religions enable their participants to:

1. mine the depths of their sacred teachings until they reach their central core; i.e., personal and direct experiences with their own Soul and internal glimpses of the state of God;

2. develop higher qualities of ethical behavior and lifestyle (is my choice good for me and all others?). Ethical conduct allows the mind to rest. From a resting position, it is able to focus and concentrate;

3. transform their emotions and slowly relinquish holding on excessively to negative emotions (fear, anger, jealousy, etc.);

4. move through life with clearer motivations; to shift away from needless attractions and to move up in the hierarchy of needs as identified by Abraham Maslow:

   • Self-Actualization
   • Self-Esteem
   • Love and Belongingness
   • Basic Physiological Needs
   • Safety and Security Needs

Our lower needs usually have to be filled before needs higher in the hierarchy become very important;

5. improve our awareness and conscientiousness; and

6. cultivate authentic wisdom.

For many, the move away from consuming (symbolically speaking) the restaurant, menus, waiters or waitresses, toward spiritual food, represents an immense shift in perspective.

One of the steps in making this drastic shift — moving within one's religion into the very heart of Wisdom — is to give yourself permission to revise your ideas about who you think you are. When we are exclusively or primarily involved in everyday, normal, non-spiritual thinking, we usually consider ourselves to be physical bodies, with brains and minds, that may or may not contain a soul.

What I am advocating is the reverse: to begin thinking of ourselves as Souls who have physical bodies. With this shift, we come to see our bodies not as our entire self, but as temporary vehicles designed for experiencing and learning on earth. This transformation in thinking is the first step in allowing ourselves an intimate relationship with the deepest core of our being — that God-like part of us that is accessible behind our mind and thoughts.

When we make this shift, some of the things that happen are that:

- we come to experience Divine companionship;
- we come to realize that even though we are not the totality of Almighty God, nevertheless, we are a powerful enough Divine fragment so as to have participated fully — actively and with free will — in choosing all of our own deep structures.

We are not cleverly built robots with the illusion of free will. We have participated in choosing the experiences and environments that developed our internal urges that drew us to choose certain paths of experience.

In viewing relationships through the lens of Spirituality:

- we come to know that all experience is a teacher and friend rather than an intrusion or an enemy;
- we come to experience Divinity;

Our fragment of Divinity is such a powerful creator that it brings us the teacher(s) we need in each moment in order to wake us up so we can further grow up.

Sometimes we draw to ourselves hope, encouragement, comfort, or inspiration; other times we select fear, terror, depression, or hopelessness. Whatever our Divinity picks, it becomes a catalyst for change and a potential for growth;

- we become more patient.

Those who practice spiritual wholeness through self-nourishment do many of the following:

- They face and address their internal injuries (which can lead to bad habits and/or addictions). They don't expect their partners to do this for them.
- They take care of their physical bodies.
- They take a few minutes, nearly every day, to sit quietly and pray and meditate. Praying usually means speaking with God while meditation means listening to God.

If you are unfamiliar with prayer, here is an easy way to begin. Pray each of the following prayers three or four times before proceeding to the next prayer. The first time through, pray these prayers for yourself. The second time through, pray them for the person in your life that is causing you the most trouble, anger, or distress.

May I be free from fear.

May_____be free from fear.

May I be filled with love.

May_____ be filled with love.

May I be filled with joy.

May_____ be filled with joy.

May I be filled with peace.

May_____ be filled with peace.

May I be filled with patience.

May_____ be filled with patience.

May I be filled with kindness.

May_____ be filled with kindness.

May I be filled with goodness.

May_____ be filled with goodness.

May I be filled with faithfulness.

May_____be filled with faithfulness.

May I be filled with gentleness.

May_____be filled with gentleness.

May I be filled with self-control.

May_____ be filled with self-control.

- They read the scriptures and accompanying books, articles, and journals of their religion.
- When needed, they make use of other spiritually oriented programs such as The Twelve Steps developed by Alcoholics Anonymous.

If you are unfamiliar with the twelve steps, here they are:

1. We admitted we were powerless over (our addiction) — that our lives had become unmanageable.

2. We came to believe that a Power greater than ourselves could restore us to sanity.

3. We made a decision to turn our will and our lives over to the care of That Higher Power, as we understood It/Him/Her.

4. We made a searching and fearless moral inventory of ourselves.

5. We admitted to That Higher Power, to ourselves, and to another human being the exact nature of our wrongs.

6. We were entirely ready to have That Higher Power remove all of our defects of character.

7. We humbly asked That Higher Power to remove our short comings.

8. We made a list of all persons we had harmed, and became willing to make amends to them all.

9. We made direct amends to such people wherever possible, except when to do so would injure them or others.

10. We continued to take a personal inventory and when we were wrong promptly admitted it.

11. We sought, through prayer and meditation, to improve our conscious contact with That Higher Power, as we understood It/Him/Her, praying only for knowledge of Its will for us and the power to carry that out.

12. Having had a spiritual awakening as the result of these steps, we tried to carry this message to all addicts — and those who act compulsively — and to practice these principles in all our affairs.

(The philosophical foundation of the Twelve Steps come from "The Sermon on the Mount, the Thirteenth chapter of First Corinthians, and the Book of James." *Pass It On*, Alcoholics Anonymous World Services, NY., N.Y. p. 147.)

- They associate with like-minded folks — in church, synagogue, temple, or other gatherings.
- They take a few minutes, nearly every day, to sit quietly and contemplate life; Why am I here? Am I wasting my life? Am I using my time well?
- They make a conscious effort to practice their religion/faith/way of life.
- Many write and use affirmations.

SPIRITUAL AFFIRMATIONS

I am free from all forms of destructive fear.

Deep within I have the deep sense of peace of mind that I've been looking for all my life.

I have found the Kingdom of God within myself.

I am living at my full potential.

I am living as God intended me to live.

I have the same sense of care and good will for others as I have for myself.

I am an energized, free, spontaneous Child of God who delivers to my world the health and healing that we all so richly deserve.

I am inner-directed, outwardly aware, properly organized, and I have a well-regulated sense of responsibility.

I am experiencing a deep sense of peace and a quiet confidence that God is leading all of Creation toward completion at just the right rate of speed.

Today will be one of the greatest days of my life.

- Many are students of their dreams — both day-dreams and night-dreams.

Susan Sims Smith, LCSW writes:
"While dreaming we are being held in the hand of God. Dreaming is tremendously creative, it is greatly personal, highly individualized, and perfectly tailored to the life of the dreamer. The Spirit that creates our dreams knows us better than we know ourselves, better than any therapists, minister, or lover could know us. The Spirit who creates the dreams is the highest IQ point anywhere, the most loving, and offers the most wisdom. As we develop a creative relationship with our dreams, we are truly being created by God. Dreams are sacred material. Most of the dreams that come are showing us how to live daily life."

Personal mental and spiritual health are the foundations of a healthy individual. Suggesting, in any way, that we can and should cover up our psychological wounds with Scripture reading and prayer is not sound advice. The entire package is necessary; i.e., good psychological health must go hand in hand with good spiritual practices. Without this level of individual health, any social and communication skills we attain will be undermined.

191

Instructions regarding spiritual practices are identical to the instructions given when putting together a thousand-piece puzzle. The instructions are simple but doing the puzzle takes a great deal of patience and concentration.

This then is the menu I handed Steve. It is my hope that it will be as useful to you as it was to him.

WRITE THAT LETTER

Notes from Chapter 10

NEARLY TWENTY YEARS AGO, Bob Hoffmann, author of *No One Is To Blame*, introduced me to therapeutic letters.

The letters I wrote to my mother, grandmother, sister, and former wife were rather mundane but they did their job; they put me in touch with some thoughts and feelings I had buried.

It was another matter when I sat down to write to my father. I remember saying, "This will be short and sweet." The reason was that he died when I was but five years of age.

My parents had been approved to serve as missionaries in South Africa. A few weeks before my parents, my sister, Gloria, and I were to leave "for the mission field," my father died of a heart attack while riding in a Los Angeles street car. It was because I had so few memories of him that I surmised, incorrectly, that there wouldn't be much to say.

The letter to my father turned out to be the longest, most vicious letter I've ever written. It was packed with sarcasm, disappointment, rage, and judgment. Until those moments, I never suspected how I really felt.

As I wrote to him, it was as if I had returned to being five and it was as if he had died days earlier. My writing style and language were adult but I was raging from a feeling level of a five-year-old whose father had left him on purpose.

My adult understanding that "he was the victim of an unexpected and unwanted heart attack" disappeared during those moments. All I was feeling and writing was the outrage of having been unfairly abandoned.

I said things like, (I've actually cleaned up my language here): "You coward! What got into your mind that caused you to leave Mom with two kids to raise? Why did you take off when the going got tough? Couldn't you have had the decency to at least leave her with some money?" Page after page, I raged on and on and on.

I have never come across a technique that is so helpful in getting in touch with any hidden emotional garbage we might, unknowingly, be carrying with us.

STEP ONE: Before starting, remind yourself of two things:

1. *A therapeutic letter is a letter you write but never send.*

The purpose of this letter is not to do damage or to get back at your partner. The purpose is to get everything out in the open so you can see, feel, and understand it. It is appropriate when writing a therapeutic letter to use violent language and give graphic details about the type of physical harm you would like to do.

Violence is only appropriate during extreme emergencies. However, it is critical in our self-understanding to know if violence is an option we crave or are considering. Uncovering our hidden thoughts and fantasies about violence is one of the first steps in preventing it.

2. *A therapeutic letter is a letter you write but never under any circumstances show to anyone.*

While writing, if you suspect that someday you will share your letter with someone, you will censor it in some way. The only way you can give yourself permission "to tell the whole truth and nothing but the truth, so help me God!" is for you to assure yourself that no one will ever read your letter.

STEP TWO: With these two things in mind, you are now ready to begin writing.

Simply start; begin writing. Don't edit, don't censor, let it all hang out, say it all, express it anyway it comes to you, feel free for once in your life to say it the way you are thinking and feeling within.

193

STEP THREE: Find a safe place to store the letter: a place where no one will find it.

STEP FOUR: Allow several days or weeks to pass, then reread it. Add whatever needs to be added until there is nothing more to say.

STEP FIVE: If you choose to share some of the information (not the letter itself) you've uncovered, rewrite those parts. Before sharing the rewritten information with your partner, share it with your clergy, or some professional listener.

STEP SIX: In the presence of that professional listener, with great consideration and care for your partner, and in as skilled manner as you can, share whatever information is critical.

STEP SEVEN: When you have done all of the above, burn your therapeutic letter while saying a prayer that God will enable you to heal from the guilt, rage, or whatever has infected you.

I close this subject by listing a litany to therapeutic letters.

Writing therapeutic letters is: a way of showing myself that I love myself, a gift I give myself, a way of taking care of myself, an emotional volcanic eruption, a way of getting to know my undiscovered, hidden, and hiding selves (our internal sub-personalities often predecease our physical death, and, new sub-personalities are continually forming so there are always infants within).

This is an effective way of "getting down," of "coming clean," of "putting all of my cards on the table face up," a way to express it all — from my greatest joy and wildest fantasy to my deepest fear, anger, and rage, a way of taking an internal shower, a way of confessing my sins and everything about which I feel guilty — all without anyone ever finding out.

It is a way to clear away all cob-webs that have collected in my mind, heart, gut, or imagination regarding any person, place, or experience, a way of traveling within my mind and performing an internal excavation of hidden memories, thoughts, and feelings. It is internal inspection by self-disclosure, a way of opening up my mind, looking into every nook and cranny, and revealing to myself all of the secrets I've been keeping from myself.

If you are not skilled at writing you may instead choose to express your fears, rage, anger, and frustrations to skilled listeners before expressing them to your partner.

Your partner deserves to know the truth about how you think and feel. They do not deserve to be attacked with verbal or emotional battering or violent language.

With all of this said, here are the details of how you can use a technique other than therapeutic letters to nourish intimacy between you and your partner.

The easiest place to do this is on a couch. One person sits upright while the other person lies in a reclining position with his head on his partner's lap. The person who is lying in the reclining position must feel comfortable. Therefore, he decides which direction he will face. He may face toward or away from his partner. Some people feel uncomfortable, confined, or simply "put on the spot" while facing their partner.

The responsibility of the partner who is sitting upright is to support and hold his partner. He supports his partner in three ways:

1. By supporting his partner's head on his/her lap.

2. By supporting his partner with his/her arms.

3. By not talking at all.

That's right. The person who has been sitting in the upright position remains silent because, in this situation, silence is the crucial foundation of support.

He says not a single word until his partner declares that he/she is complete. At that point, the partner who is sitting upright says two words and two words only — "thank you."

When both partners are sitting up or on their feet, the one who has been lying in the prone position may wish to talk further. If he/she wishes to or not is their business. *That person alone must be left with that decision.*

TELL THE TRUTH

Notes from Chapter 11

THESE FOUR QUESTIONS will help you see if this suggestion (Tell The Truth As Soon As Possible) applies to you.

1. Do you often avoid talking about important issues, or withdraw from such conversations altogether?

   ❏ YES   ❏ NO

2. Do you find that routine discussions erupt into destructive communications?

   ❏ YES   ❏ NO

3. Do you feel your partner is frequently turning what you say into something negative, or something you didn't mean?

   ❏ YES   ❏ NO

4. Do you feel as if your partner often either disregards what you say or puts down your efforts or opinions?

   ❏ YES   ❏ NO

If you have answered "yes" to any of these questions, a warning light should have just gone on. If you have answered "yes" to all of them, you are well on your way toward divorce.

Today is the time to seek outside help.

LEARN ABOUT ONE ANOTHER

Notes from Chapter 12

TWENTY-FIVE YEARS AGO when our son, Sean, was born to my first wife and me, we were given a book that detailed the stages of development in children. Each time we used it, which we did for many years, we could see that he was either a month or so ahead or a month or so behind the norm.

That information was both helpful and comforting in our day-to-day dealing with him, knowing that his skills, attitudes, and actions were normal. Being first-time parents, it is a vast understatement to say there was a great deal we didn't know about children. (Speaking for myself, after having raised him, there still is.)

Raising him was not unlike what I imagine it might be like raising an alien who dropped in from a different planet. However, that book gave us the exact information we needed at the time. To this day, I am deeply grateful to whoever gave us that book.

In addition to the news and sports, some of my favorite television programs are the nature shows. Time after time I've heard the narrator emphasize the importance of understanding an animal if we are to protect it. One example is Jean Goodall who, for more than three decades, has observed chimpanzees. The insights she has gained and shared with the rest of us are preventing the extinction of chimps.

For as long as I've been asking men questions about women I have heard statements like, "George, don't even try. You will never understand how a woman thinks." "Give it up; as soon as you have them figured out, they change." "George, all they want to do is trap you into marriage and then talk you to death."

I also have overheard women complaining about men. The general complaints are, "He won't talk." "He doesn't listen; he only gives advice." "He likes sports and his hobby more than me." "He will never tell me how he feels; he only tells me what he thinks."

The point I'm making is this: if we wish to get along well with members of the opposite sex, and I believe we can no longer afford not to, we will have to study one another.

MEN VS. WOMEN - BASHING

For as long as I've been aware, women have accused men of "not being in touch with their feelings." Men have struck back by saying that "women talk too much." These are old myths that need to be dispelled.

When men and women are video-taped discussing, arguing, and fighting, and at the same time, sensors have been attached to monitor their heart rate, blood pressure, and perspiration, the conclusion is revealing.

During a typical confrontation, the pulse in men is faster, their blood pressure is higher, and they sweat more. Their body and facial language, as well as the tone of their voice and the words they choose, also indicate that they are feeling more distress than their female counterpart.

The conclusion is clear: men do feel their feelings and they express them, too. The fact that they don't talk about them is natural because talking is not how men dispel their emotions and it is not how they seek intimacy. Men dispel their emotions through activities - hobbies, sports, work, projects, etc.

When men reach excitement during a negotiation, or game, or activity and when they reach rage during a fight, war, or other times of danger, they are feeling so intensely that they can barely stand it. They act out their intense feelings often with aggression and crude brutality accompanied by, what is natural for them, the appropriate amount of words.

MOST MEN ARE "IN TOUCH"
WITH THEIR EMOTIONS

Most men are "in touch" with their emotions. The fact that talking is not the primary, chosen, or comfortable playing field for most men (by and large, the average woman in America says twice as many words each day as does the average man) has allowed women to get away with their claim that men are not in touch with their feelings.

By saying this, women often mean, "men don't feel soft feelings," or, "men don't talk about soft feelings." These are far different from the false generalization that "men are not in touch with their feelings."

Men talk as much as women when they are with someone they trust and respect.

Women have been as unfairly accused by men as much as men have been unfairly accused by women. "Women talk too much" is unfair. Both men and women talk as much as they need to. By talking, women are seeking intimacy. By doing things, men are seeking intimacy.

Both biologically and culturally, women have been given permission to express the softer emotions. However, generally women often experience difficulty in expressing the harsher emotions or feelings of anger.

Both biologically and culturally, men have been given permission to express the harsher emotions. Generally men are encouraged to "be strong" and restrain themselves from the expressions of painful emotions.

Now we need to move to a place where everyone can express all of their emotions without penalty.

Men and women need to stop bashing one another. Bashing needs to be replaced with sensitive caring, and an acceptance and celebration that the opposite sex is different.

FURTHER READING

Embracing Each Other, Relationship as Teacher, Healer & Guide, Hal Stone, Ph.D. & Sidra Winkelman, Ph.D., Natarij, 1989

Fire In The Belly: On Being a Man, Sam Keen, Bantam. Keen denounces war, work, and sexual prowess as adequate rites of male passage. He insists that old gender sex differences are simply wrong. Being a sensitive man is not paramount to being a "worm-boy" or wimp.

Iron John: A Book About Men, Robert Bly, Addison-Wesley. His message is "men need to learn from other men." Using a heroic figure from a myth, Bly urges men to find, create, or become a "mentor-like initiator and source of divine energy."

GIVE DELIGHTFUL SURPRISES

Notes from Chapter 16

WHEN ONE HIGHLY SUCCESSFUL couple was interviewed, the woman indicated that unexpected surprises added "spice" to their marriage. She said, "I expect to receive a gift for my birthday, our anniversary, and Christmas, but what delights me more are the small surprises during the year."

Some people hate surprise parties but everyone, at least secretly, appreciates small, unnecessary, thoughtful gifts and gestures.

I'm not suggesting anything elaborate, or expensive. As a way to get your creative juices going, here are a few ideas:

- Bring something home for each person in the family that will say, "I've been thinking about you while I've been away." Perhaps a cookie, flower, or card.
- Phone during the day, especially when it is unnecessary.
- Prepare your partner's favorite meal.

Some things I will do are: _____

_____

TAKE TIME TO BE ALONE

Notes from Chapter 19

M Y WIFE, LINDA, is a United Airlines flight attendant. She began working for United before we met. We met about seventeen years ago and have been married now for thirteen. The pattern of her being away either overnight or for several days is normal for me; I've never know anything different.

I enjoy my time alone. It allows me to do as I wish without wondering if Linda would want to do it with me or not. I have a particular leather jacket that she doesn't like. She also is not fond of raw fish. So, while she is away, sometimes I put on that leather jacket and go to one of my favorite Japanese restaurants. This is one of the ways we both win.

Also, because most of my work schedule is determined by appointments rather than regular office hours, when she is away I work long hours and line up appointments one after another. When she is in town, I try and have as much free time as possible. This isn't always possible, but it has been working well for both of us now for all these years.

ESTABLISH LIFE GOALS

Notes from Chapter 20

T HERE ARE SEVERAL WAYS of getting clear about what you want to do with your life.

One way is to write stories about your life. Or, write stories about your death; i.e., an obituary. In these fantasy stories, you may discover what you always wanted to do but did not have the courage to pursue. You can make collages together as a part of your household council (Chapter 32).

To make a collage, get a few magazines and cut out pictures and words that indicate how you want your marriage to be. Paste them on a piece of cardboard and display it in a convenient place. As you look at it from time to time, you will become clearer and clearer about what you want both out of life and out of your relationships.

PREPARE FOR DEATH

Notes from Chapter 21

W HAT WOULD YOU PUT on your own tombstone? Here is your chance to do so.

_____

_____

_____

_____

_____

_____

_____

_____

_____

_____

WRITING YOUR OWN OBITUARY is a way of gaining self-knowledge. I suggest writing it twice.

The first time it is for you and you alone. Knowing that no one but you will ever read it will help keep the censuring part of your mind quieter. Your obituary should include everything about you that needs to be said.

The second time is an edited version. This is the one you will show and share with your partner. Writing two versions will also provide you with insights about how safe you feel with your partner. The emotions that this exercise will evoke are great teachers.

You might want to include your place of birth, the names of your parents, siblings, husband/wife and children. And your education, vocation, jobs you've had, clubs or groups you belonged to, hobbies, accomplishments, failures, traits, and your secrets. Write about accidents, operations, and the funniest moments of your life. Include your dreams, hopes, and plans that never happened, the four or five most impressive, helpful, or mind-stretching people you've met, books you read, and experiences you've had. Write what your philosophy of life was. Why were you here and did you accomplish your purpose? Write about your most meaningful moments. Finally, make up a few quotes that you hope your closest friends will say.

My Obituary Should Read...

born _____   died _____

Today,_____

_____

_____

_____

_____

Services will be conducted at _____

_____

Donations should be made to _____

_____

_____

A To-do List — In Preparation For My Death

❏ Make peace with God.

❏ Make peace with others:

_____

_____

_____

_____

❏ Write letters — to be mailed upon my death — to:

_____

_____

_____

_____

❏ Make a will; i.e., get my financial house in order.

❏ Leave specific details about the distribution of my stuff.

❏ Leave funeral and burial instructions with the church/synagogue or attorney's office.

❏ Prepare for the worst:

   ❏ A living will

   ❏ Power of attorney

RECOMMENDED BOOKS

Re: Death & Near Death Experiences

Grace and Grit, Spirituality and Healing in the Life and Death of Treya Killam Wilber, Ken Wilber, Shambhala, Boston, 1993. A book written by Ken and his wife and her struggle to find a cure for her cancer.

The Trip of a Lifetime, Greg Palmer, A four-hour video series on PBS, October, 1993. "Death, not space, is the final frontier and unlike any other frontier; death is the one we all have to go to one day. So what follows is a journey of reconnaissance by looking at the way people all over the world prepare for life's last great adventure, we hope to get some sense of the adventure itself. It's a journey of grief, joy, fear, and hope. It's the trip of a lifetime."

Death and Grief, A Guide for Clergy, Alan D. Wolfelt, Accelerated Development Inc. Muncie, Indiana, 1988. Don't let the "clergy" in the title scare you. This book will be helpful to anyone experiencing a death of any kind. Without a doubt, this is the best book of its kind I've ever read.

Embraced by The Light, Betty J. Eadie, Gold Leaf Press, Placerville, CA, 1992. "The beautiful message: Love is supreme...Love must govern...We create our own surroundings by the thoughts we think...We are sent here to live life fully, to live it abundantly, to find joy in our own creations, to experience both failure and success, to use free will to expand and magnify our lives...We are to be kind, to be tolerant, to give generous service." p. ix

Emmanuel's Book & Emmanuel's Book II, Pat Rodegast and Judith Stanton, Bantam Books, New York. The main message is: death is safe. Both books have excellent chapters on death.

Journeys Out Of The Body, Robert Monroe, New York, 1971.

Life After Life, Raymond Moody. The first modern, popular book recording Near-Death Experiences.

Many Lives, Many Masters, Brian L. Weiss, M.D., Simon & Schuster, New York, 1988. The true story of a prominent psychiatrist, his young patient, and the past-life therapy that changed both their lives.

Testimony of Light, Helen Greaves, Neville and Spierman, Essex, England.

The Challenging Light, Helen Greaves, Neville and Spierman, Suffux, England.

The Tibetan Book Of The Living And Dying, Sogyal Rinpoche, Harper, San Francisco, 1992. How to help the dying, both practically and spiritually. "...we cannot hope to die peacefully if our lives have been full of violence, or if our minds have mostly been agitated by emotions like anger, attachment, or fear. So if we wish to die well, we must learn how to live well: Hoping for a peaceful death, we must cultivate peace in our mind, and in our way of life." p. ix.

The Sacred Art of Dying, Kenneth Kramer, Paulist Press, 1988. "Religious traditions ritualize the death process to remind us of the impermanence of life, and that whatever lies on the other side of death is as real, if not infinitely more so, than life itself. These rituals offer mourners a sense of victory over death, a way to dance on the dome of death."

The Worshipbook, Westminster Press, Philadelphia, 1970. Witness to the Resurrection, pages 71-88. A collection of bible passages recommended for use by those grieving.

Transformed By The Light & Closer To The Light, Melvin Morse, M.D. Morse coined the term "zestaholics" for the voracious appetites for accomplishment of those who return to physical life. They are delighted, happy folks who are taking every advantage that physicality offers. They are some of the happiest and more productive folks alive.

LIVE FULLY

Notes from Chapter 22

MANY YEARS AGO I went to a private home to meet with a family in order to prepare for a funeral. There were about twenty family members present, which was an unusually large group. The widower was wealthy in nearly every way, but confessed openly that he had one regret. For a number of years his wife had wanted to buy a particular house. He said that he could easily have afforded it, but had procrastinated for unknown reasons.

About six months earlier he had finally consented to buy it, and now the renovations were nearly complete. He said, "That is my only regret. I wish I had bought that home ten years ago. She never got to live in her dream home."

At that time, my wife, Linda, and I had located a home we both wanted. It was expensive and we were both unclear if we could really afford it. Following the meeting with that family, as I drove back to the church, I determined that we would get that house. I remembering saying to myself, "Linda or I may be dead in six months, so go for it." We did!

In his books about near death experience, *Transformed by The Light* and *Closer to The Light*, Melvin Morse, M.D. coined the term "zestaholic." Zestaholics have voracious appetites for accomplishment when they return to physical health. They are delighted, happy folks who are taking every advantage that physicality offers. They are some of the happiest and most productive folks alive.

These findings are echoed in *Other World Journeys, Accounts of Near-Death Experience in Medieval and Modern Times* by Carol Zaleski. Oxford University Press, Oxford, 1987. Her book is one of the most scholarly works available and it also has a wonderful bibliography.

"...near-death subjects say they are attracted to a new focus of irresistible interest, another world more real than the one they left behind...survivors of mystical near-death experience neither run to a monastery nor run off a cliff; their expressions of apparent zest for death are accompanied by great appreciation of physical life."

"Indeed, a life-affirming outlook is the central message of near-death narratives."

The happiest people I know are people who are "out there," "doing their thing," pursuing their dream and living life to its fullest. When you join us, you will add to your relationship a zest that is unattainable any other way.

What are you waiting for?

ENABLE THE NEEDY

Notes from Chapter 23

T HERE ARE SEVERAL EASY WAYS to become involved in helpful community activities. You could begin at no better place than to read together, *Random Acts Of Kindness*, Conari Press, Berkeley, CA. 1993. A summary of its message is found on its back cover:

"Imagine what would happen if there were an outbreak of kindness in the world, if everybody did one kind thing on a daily basis. This book will inspire you to start with the small, the particular, the individual — to bring delight and goodness to yourself and others." This beautiful and simple book is packed with things to do for others.

A second way to begin is to call your local volunteer bureau. If you live in a place that is too small for such a bureau, you can volunteer at your local school, hospital, library, church, temple, synagogue, or civic or social club. Happy couples reach out and touch others.
I would enjoy helping others by:

_____

_____

_____

_____

_____

_____

_____

_____

ESTABLISH RULES

Notes from Chapter 24

I F YOU ARE IN THE HABIT of arguing or fighting, here is a simple tool to help you replace that bad habit with a good habit. The more angry we are, the more structure we need. If you have not used them already, now is a good time to practice using the two worksheets — The Speaker's Page and The Listener's Page — found on pages 174–177. They will give you a framework. If you are willing to stay within that framework and practice the habits of those who are skilled at conflict-management, you, like them, will succeed. By success, I mean that both you and your partner will get more of what you want.

DON'T LIE

Notes from Chapter 27

I AM OFTEN ASKED whether I believe that a couple should "confess" their past sins to one another. Confessing to our partner is problematic. Sometimes confessions are used as a way of getting back at our partner. Often confession relieves our guilt, but at the same time it builds a wall between us. It usually places a burden on one of us.

In general, I advise against such unveilings. If an individual is severely bothered by some past "sin," I believe he should first discuss it with a chaplain or clergyperson. I have a great deal more trust in confessions made in private, and then to God, than I do in confessions made by married partners, one to the other.

Secondly, prior to confessing to his mate, he should speak with an experienced and sensitive therapist. If there is uncertainty that confessing would bring healing, listening to the advice of a chaplain or therapist would be helpful. If such a confession is necessary, I suggest that it be made to the partner in the presence of the chaplain or therapist.

One final word of caution. Even married persons have a right to their own secrets. Probing for secrets is not done by couples who have long, healthy relationships. Each person's right to privacy is respected. We can begin identifying our own secrets by making a mental list of those things we have been, and perhaps still are, unwilling to tell our partner.

KEEP YOUR WORD

Notes from Chapter 28

ONE OF THE FIRST THINGS military people learn is that team-work is essential to survival and lack of team-work is a killer. Each person's doing his/her job, with the confidence that every other person is doing so as well, insures the best results.

Similarly, in our personal relationships, even though the results are not immediately lethal, breaking agreements can be devastating. When we make an agreement to do something or be somewhere at a certain time, and we fail to keep our agreement, our partner loses a small portion of confidence in us. To be sure, not every broken agreement is a life and death matter, but having a habit of breaking agreements builds up distrust and resentment, just as grains of sand can build into huge dunes.

At some point, we've taken as much as we are willing to take. Then, an explosion occurs, fueled by fear or anger, and we find our-selves in the middle of a raging, blinding storm. Such storms can be avoided. They can be avoided if we replace our poor habits with good habits, such as:

• We should make only the agreements that we intend to keep.

  If we are living with persons who are controllers, manipulators, or are more highly skilled at arguing than we are, there is a tendency to "agree to whatever they want just to get on with life."

• We need to change the agreement as soon as possible when we realize that we cannot keep it. Even if we will be only ten minutes late, making a call to inform them is important. Such considera-tion builds trust. Not calling when we will be late is being insensi-tive, as well as taking advantage of the other person. It is a form of battering, because it is controlling our partners' time.

- When the persons are not available for renegotiating and we break the agreement, when we do get together, we must take whatever time is needed to "reconnect" with those persons. Take whatever time is needed to let them express their true feelings, fantasies of accidents or deaths, of how worried they were, phone calls they made, etc. They need to get it all out, not only part of it.

- Each year we make several hundred agreements with our partner. Most couples have made some promise regarding marital vows, being late or early, sticking by a budget, doing what was promised: picking up the children, bringing something home from the store. Breaking an agreement builds distrust between partners.

- Keeping agreements builds *TRUST* and *SAFETY*.

- There is no such thing as "a meaningless broken agreement."

The following sentences *do not heal* the damage done by a broken agreement:

- "Don't get so worked up over this, it's not the end of the world."

- "You know I'm always late so what difference does it make."

- "You knew I was coming."

- "Who do you think you are, being so upset with me?"

The following sentences *are helpful* in starting the healing process:

- "I know you must be worked up over this. Even though it is not the end of the world, let me explain." "... I'm sorry for ..."

- "I know that was thoughtless..." "I'll make no excuses. Next time I'll call."

- "You probably thought I wasn't coming."

- "You have a right to be upset with me. I broke our agreement."

DON'T PARENT YOUR PARTNER

Notes from Chapter 29

TO PHIL AND JILL I described the following word picture of how I saw them treating each other. I said that if I were to visualize their method of communication in cartoon form, I would draw two dog owners meeting on the street. As they attempt to pass, both dogs leap into action wanting to get at the other dog's throat. In order to keep them apart, the owners must lean backward and hold onto their leashes with both hands. They must use all of their strength to hold back their angry dogs who are pulling so hard on their chains, that they are choking.

Fortunately, they both laughed. I asked them to keep this illustration in mind as we continued to talk. For the next few minutes they were on their best behavior, but I could see that it was killing them to remain silent while the other spoke. Soon, they were at it again.

I recommended that they come to see me again, separately. She refused. He agreed. I suspect that he agreed only because she refused.

DON'T ASSUME MIND-READING

Notes from Chapter 30

THE INITIAL, EMOTIONAL onslaught of love/lust stimulates our entire beings. Nearly everything is turned on, wide open, all at once. We are happy and able to do with little sleep. Our work becomes easy and the day passes quickly. Our thoughts, rather than wandering, are focused. We are more like SuperMan or WonderWoman than normal.

Our love/lust experience leads us to unsurpassed generosity and grandiose promises and day-dreams that lead to thoughts, hopes, and plans that are exaggerated. We express our most elaborate dreams, which are usually believed literally by our partner at the moment.

Later on, we are often held to those dreams, hopes, plans, and promises. Nevertheless, the experience of love/lust *is* all that it is "cracked up" to be.

Love is the wonderful world of lazy, rambling rivers of emotion which sometimes cascade, become waterfalls, white water, and rapids-like. It is fantastic and none of us should miss it. But, watch out! Just around the corner, this river always slows down.

Under the initial glow of love/lust all of our abilities are heightened. We can nearly read our partners' mind. We seem to know automatically when they want to make love, to have dinner, go to a movie, hold hands, cuddle, go for a walk or run, have a picnic, or whatever. At this stage, "mind-reading" is the easiest, most normal thing in the world.

Eventually, these emotions will settle down, for just as it is impossible to run full speed all the time, so it is impossible to retain such a high level of emotional love/lust. It is then that we resume our normal patterns and return to being "merely human." It is at this point — when everyday living begins — that this sort of trouble starts.

The more realistic way of looking at this is to understand that, within each of us, there is often a "fantasy partner." This fantasy may have originated in childhood when we idealized someone — usually our mother, father, grandparent, etc. When we marry, we often unconsciously overlay this childhood fantasy onto our partner. Most of us, at some deep level, marry people who remind us of our mother, father, grandparent, aunt, uncle, etc. We do this primarily because we recognize in them something familiar (which makes them seem safe) and appealing.

Unnoticed and unacknowledged fantasies treat us like prisoners. They drive us in strange and exaggerated ways. They are the fuel that feeds unrealistic dreams and demands of our partner. The cure for this begins with our acknowledgment of these ideas as fantasies and that our expectations of our partner are unrealistically high.

The most certain way to bring balance to our expectations is to report our desires as accurately as possible.

An almost certain way to ruin your marriage is to tell your partner half the story and then demand that they should have been smart enough or intuitive enough, or know you well enough, to have figured it out.

213

An almost certain way to strengthen your marriage is to communicate skillfully, which means that they don't have to guess about what you meant.

DON'T COMPETE

Notes from Chapter 31

PEOPLE WHO CONSIDER their partner a competitor answer "no" to questions such as: Do I feel safe living with this person? Is it safe to express my opinions? Is it safe to be emotional? Is there enough for both of us? Do you feel that you must beat your partner, even while playing?

The emotional ingredient that infects a relationship, making it unhealthy, is the feeling of a lack of safety. Those who see their partner as an enemy consider him/her to be less important than they see themselves. Trust and safety are missing when in one another's presence.

The emotional ingredient that is the foundation of a healthy relationship is the feeling of safety.

HOLD HOUSEHOLD COUNCILS

Notes from Chapter 32

Some of the basics of the Council are:

1. HOLD A REGULAR MEETING
   For the first few months, it is wise to hold a council meeting on a regular schedule — weekly, bi-weekly, or once a month. As time goes on, the household itself can determine how often such a meeting needs to occur.

2. SHARE THE CHAIR

Everyone in the household takes a turn at being the moderator. Even very young children, with a little help, can serve in this capacity. This allows the children to practice taking leadership roles within a safe environment. If grandparents are present, the fact that they may not hear very well or may forget the agenda is welcomed because their reduced capacity is a part of the present condition of the household.

3. EVERYONE IN THE HOUSEHOLD NEEDS TO BE PRESENT

This includes the pets. Pets are often a source of pleasure as well as problems. If they are absent from the meeting, the atmosphere of the household changes. This is also true of new infants and elderly grandparents. To be sure, in some cases the meeting would run smoother without them, but their presence assures that the social environmental atmosphere of the household remains intact. The council should also take place in the home because problems need to be addressed at the location where the problems occur.

4. RECORD AGREEMENTS

Just as everyone takes turns as moderator, so everyone (almost) can take notes. Again, even very young children can serve as recording secretary with a little help. Agreements are written because it is normal for different people to hear different things. When it is written, at least some of the disagreement is handled.

5. CONCLUDE YOUR MEETING BY DOING SOMETHING FUN

Start the meeting with an agreement about how to conclude the meeting. Popcorn and soft drinks while watching a crazy movie cannot end every meeting but it's a good start.

MAKE HISTORY TOGETHER

Notes from Chapter 34

THESE SCRIPTS and other influences, some known and others vague, make up our internal scripts. Eventually, our internal scripts becomes our personal scripture unless we tap into our Soul and clean up the mess from there (See Chapter 9, *Feed Your Soul*).

Our personal scripture directs our lives. Everyone is directed by his own scripture. If our private script/scriptures are causing pain to ourselves and to others, it is essential that we change it.

Do you know the contents of your Family Script/Scriptures?

Many happy people do and they are making a conscious effort to emulate the positive attributes and eliminate the negative traits that have been passed on to them.

I have gotten a great deal of insight into the patterns imprinted, impressed, imposed, and passed on to me by my parents and other family members. I have gotten this insight primarily from two sources.

A Genogram is a genealogy that includes not only the names, dates, and relationships of our family members (our family tree) but also includes their habits, their accomplishments and failures, as well as the emotional quality of their relationships within the family.

For example, I learned that the men in my family have had a tendency, in some way, to abandon their family. Some abandonment occurred by their walking away while others stayed on the scene. They provided food and shelter, but were unavailable emotionally or intellectually. I reproduced this tendency by becoming a work-a-holic. We work-a-holics abandon our families. We leave them for the bright green pastures of work. My son, Sean, and I have talked often about this tendency. We are making a conscious effort not to continue this negative family pattern.

Another group of remarkable insights occurred when I filled out a brief but effective form called *The Strength Development Inventory* by Elias Porter. This inventory is available through any licensed counselor.

All those we encounter have a script of their own. It, therefore, must be emphasized that some of our script — which is something like an accumulation of appendixes to our ancestral and immediate family patterns — come from our greater extended family. Our greater extended family was/is our close friends whom we met at school, work, or play. It also includes all influential people such as teachers and authority figures.

References

The Paradox Of Success, When Winning At Work Means Losing At Life, John R. O'Neil, Jeremy Tarcher/Putnam, New York, 1993. Suggesting that one of the new definitions for success in the 90's is balance between vocation, home, family, friends, and community involvement.

The 7 Habits of Highly Effective People, Principle-Centered Leadership, and *First Things First,* by Stephen R. Covey.

ESTABLISH HEALTHY SYSTEMS

Notes from Chapter 35

A S HARMLESS AS IT MAY SEEM, the following chart may prove to be critical in allowing you to see one of the foundations of your disagreements. Often the foundation for disagreement is a hidden or unspoken agenda.

If, for example, the husband or male has been operating under the assumption that he is the Senior Partner and his wife or partner is a Junior Partner; i.e., they discuss things but he has the final veto/OK — and she is working under the assumption that they have an Equal Partnership — they, being on different frequencies, will keep disconnecting or being at odds but never knowing exactly why.

If this rings true for you, the problem may not be your communication skills, but your assumptions regarding what form of relationship you truly have. When you and your partner are working under different unspoken assumptions, war is inevitable.

STYLES OF MARITAL RELATIONSHIPS	
Colonial Times	*Owner/Property* Husbands had all rights, privileges, and power. Men were 90% literate, while only 10% of the women were literate. Wives did what their husbands told them to do. Husbands took over where fathers left off. The society at large supported this arrangement and duplicated it in the work-place.
1800's	*Head/Complement* Husbands were the "heads" of the family and wives were to complement him.
1920's	*Senior Partner/Junior Partner* Women began to work but made far less money. Their "junior partner" status at work was mirrored in the home. The first manuals were written on sexual satisfaction for women.
Today	*Equal Partnership* Everything is now open for negotiation and everything remains open for renegotiation forever. There is a premium on problem-solving and healthy communications. All roles are interchangeable.

IS YOUR RELATIONSHIP TYPICAL OF COLONIAL TIMES, THE 1800'S, THE 1920'S, OR TODAY?

I feel/think that our relationship is a _____ relationship.

I feel/think that my partner thinks we have a _____ relationship.

I want a _____ relationship with my partner.

ELEMENTS IN A HEALTHY RELATIONSHIP/FAMILY ARE:	ELEMENTS IN AN UNHEALTHY RELATIONSHIP/FAMILY ARE:
• shared spiritual values — truth, justice, and mercy (thoughtfulness, consideration);	• unhealthy shared values — control through brute force or manipulation, dishonesty, not getting caught, "doing one's own thing," or conflicting values;
• shared decision making;	• one person controls from a position of power — power gained through personality, physical strength, financial control, or just plain cunning.
• opportunities for children that are in keeping with their talents, needs, and family resources;	• there may be favorites while the other children are left to fend for themselves;
• budgets that are balanced while accommodating an affordable amount of debt;	• spending is determined by whoever has the power, regardless of long-term consequences of available income;
• behavior based on a value system that is kind and generous, yet disciplined.	• behavior stems from greed, selfishness and anger.

References

Getting All The Love You Want, Harvelle, Hendrix

Getting What You Want, How to Reach Agreement and Resolve Conflict Every Time, Kare Anderson, Dutton, 1993

Homecoming: Reclaiming and Championing Your Inner Child, John Bradshaw, Bantam. A book about recovery from childhood trauma. Many excellent exercises that actually do the job.

No One Is To Blame, Bob Hoffmann, Doubleday. What to do after realizing that we were raised in a dysfunctional family.

Not Tonight, Dear, Anthony Pietropinto, Double Day, New York, 1990

We Can Work It Out, Making Sense of Marital Conflict, Clifford Notarius, Ph.D., & Howard Markman, Ph.D., (G. P. Putnam's Sons, 1993.)

PREPARE FOR LOVE-MAKING

Notes from Chapter 38

WHEN WE GOT TOGETHER again, I asked each of them (Max and Jane) to take a moment and reread the paragraphs and to keep track of how they were feeling while reading. They did. Max said, "I don't know what to do." Jane said, "I feel frightened."

I mentioned that their responses proved to me that they were healthy, normal, human beings. By that I meant that, as a first response to a new idea, human males often want to spring into action and do something; human females want to talk about how they feel before proceeding.

Jane said that what frightened her was that she had never told anyone about her thoughts, fantasies, and true feelings. Her *modus operandi* had been to be, in public, what a good girl and wife was suppose to be; i.e., cooperative, productive and so forth.

Max had a similar explanation. He had bought — hook, line, and sinker — all of the cultural nonsense we place on human males to be strong, silent, self-reliant, and private in order to be all right.

In Max and Jane, we have examples of folks who were playing rigid, stylized roles as if their daily life were a required theatrical performance. The real Max and Jane were locked inside under their clothing and underneath their physical bodies.

Even though they both liked what I said and thought it was probably true, it took weeks of courageous practice for them to begin breaking their old patterns. Today, more than five years later (both are in professionally led small groups where they talk about their fears and accomplishments), they continue to find parts of themselves they are fearful to share with one another.

We're all aware of the birthing process: a physical body grows inside and, when ready, comes out. Similarly, intimacy grows from the inside out. The heart of intimacy is sharing privacy. Sharing my personal privacy means allowing my partner to know me more thoroughly than any other person on earth knows me. It is allowing her or him to see into my inner world where I feel and talk to myself.

Authentic intimacy includes sharing affection, familiarity, understandings, acceptance, openness, closeness, warm feelings, thoughtfulness, my time, attention, and possessions. It includes sharing my day dreams; i.e., my fondest wishes, deepest hopes, and wildest fantasies. It includes sharing my night dreams, those mysterious mental movies created in my internal university that reveal truths and directions I need for living my life successfully.

Changing the metaphor in a relationship: intimacy is the word that acts as an umbrella under which all other words reside. For me, the other words that have been mentioned earlier — safety, commitment, healthy and skilled communication, etc., — all dance under this word.

Intimacy is what we all secretly crave. This is not to say that everyone has the same capacity for intimacy. Just as some can take only so much of one thing or another, so it is with intimacy. The average man and the average woman seek intimacy in different ways. Women tend to have massive capacities for intimacy and they seek it by talking. Men also have massive capacities for intimacy and they seek it by doing things together, usually with other men whom they trust. Satisfying sexual experience over a long period of time requires thoughtful planning, time to organize, and time set aside so no rushing is involved.

It is my conclusion, not only when it comes to sex but to many other things, that the average woman knows more about men than the average man knows about women. One of the wisest things a man can do is to learn what a woman really wants during love-making and then provide the experience.

A common complaint about married-sex is how lazy and unthoughtful their partner has become regarding love-making. The following chart contains a few things to keep in mind:

PREPARING FOR INTIMATE LOVE-MAKING	
When preparing your partner's favorite meal, it would be good to know...	*When preparing to make love with your partner, it would be good to know...*
1. What day and time would be best for you?	1. What day and time would be best for you?
2. What do you *not* want me to prepare?	2. What do you *not* want me to do?
3. Where would you like to eat?	3. Where would you like to make love?
4. What kind of meal would you like? — a casual picnic, a romantic evening dinner, or something else?	4. What kind of sexual experience would you like now?

SPEAKER'S PAGE

The subject we have agreed to discuss is our love-life.

Answer the following questions <u>with yourself in mind</u>.
Circle how you feel right now about discussing this subject.

I feel...

afraid	angry	anxious	awful
bad	confused	crazy	dazed
delighted	disappointed	distrusted	distrustful
elated	empty	embarrassed	ecstatic
excited	exhausted	fateful	fearful
finished	frustrated	furious	good
grateful	great	happy	hopeful
hopeless	ideal	listless	lost
lousy	nearly perfect	nervous	not understood
panicked	resented	resentful	sad
satisfied	stuck	terrible	terrified
troubled	uncertain	unhappy	unimportant
unsafe	used	wasted	weary
wonderful	wronged		

(continued on page 225)

(continued from page 224)

What I want is

What I don't want is

_____

_____

_____

_____

_____

_____

_____

What I'm willing to do is

What I'm unwilling to do is

_____

_____

_____

_____

_____

_____

_____

_____

_____

(continued on page 226)

(Continued from page 225)

THE LISTENER'S PAGE

The subject we have agreed to discuss is our love-life.

Fill in this page <u>while your partner reports his/her answers to you.</u>
Circle how you feel right now about discussing this subject.

The way my partner feels about discussing this subject right now is…

afraid	angry	anxious	awful
bad	confused	crazy	dazed
delighted	disappointed	distrusted	distrustful
elated	empty	embarrassed	ecstatic
excited	exhausted	fateful	fearful
finished	frustrated	furious	good
grateful	great	happy	hopeful
hopeless	ideal	listless	lost
lousy	nearly perfect	nervous	not understood
panicked	resented	resentful	sad
satisfied	stuck	terrible	terrified
troubled	uncertain	unhappy	unimportant
unsafe	used	wasted	weary
wonderful	wronged		

(continued on page 227)

(continued from page 226)

What he/she wants is   *What he/she doesn't want is*

_____   _____

_____   _____

_____   _____

_____   _____

_____   _____

_____   _____

_____   _____

_____   _____

What he/she is willing to do is   *What he/she is unwilling to do is*

_____   _____

_____   _____

_____   _____

_____   _____

_____   _____

_____   _____

_____   _____

_____   _____

DON'T BLAME

Notes from Chapter 39

PLACING BLAME ON OTHERS for our attitudes and actions, especially if our reactions are explosive, is placing the blame where it should not be. It also robs us of the very energy we need to straighten things out.

When we accept that we are the creator, the author, the producer, the director, and the "star" of the movie of our own lives, we move into a powerful position — one of strength not force.

An enlivening thing to do is to shift from blaming other people or circumstances on our troubles and see ourselves as being in the driver's seat. When we do this, we move into an influential position: a position where we can do something about our problems.

People who are skilled at handling problems often follow a few simple steps:

- They identify the problem by name.
- They seek advice from those more experienced.
- They try one thing, and if it proves ineffective, they try something different.
- They continue seeking for a solution and they keep experimenting with possibilities until they find what works.

MANAGE YOUR MONEY

Notes from Chapter 42

TWELVE STEP PROGRAMS do not teach by lecture or by directly confronting people in public. Participants learn by listening to others tell their stories. Listeners learn by recognizing their own destructive patterns, and by practicing The Steps.

What Nash and Tracy discovered was that their overspending had roots.

They also realized the impact of being raised by parents who suffered during the Depression. When it came to spending, they had always identified their parents as "cheap." A part of their free-wheeling spending sprees was rebellion against their "tightwad" parents.

Another factor was their sizable incomes and the apparent freedom this allowed them. One of the things they discovered was that before they met they had not spent quite so freely. However, finding a partner whose secret desires were nearly identical to theirs — nearly unrestricted spending — was a real find. It somehow gave them permission to unleash their pent-up desire to spend freely.

What they also discovered was something even more primitive. It was rebellion against anyone's telling them what to do. Separately, as children, they had been held down, held back, and frustrated by over-protective parents.

Today, they are not out of debt but they continue to address their addiction together.

Counseling with them forced me to face my own spending habits. One of the pieces of wisdom I learned from them was the need for "a life-time budget," something I had never heard of before.

A life-time budget is to money what Steven Covey's concept of time-management is to daily scheduling. If you've not read his book, *First Things First*, you're in for a real treat. In it he details the disadvantages of using a clock rather than a compass in making life-choices. The clock is wonderful for short term accomplishments, but when we are married to one, we can lose sight of where we really wish to go. With a compass we can constantly check to see if we are heading in an optimal direction.

To be sure, when we are in a whirlpool-type of crisis, we must place ourselves on an extremely tight budget for a period of time. But, a far more effective way to plan our finances is to speculate about what we wish our financial condition to be when we are in our 90's. Starting there, we work backward in determining the steps needed to achieve those goals.

When making an individual or household budget, don't think only of immediate needs or of one year at a time — think in terms of a lifetime.

229

My wife and I have had many discussions but no arguments over money. There are several reasons:

1. We practice the conflict-management techniques detailed in this book.

2. Another huge factor is that we earn a near equal amount and contribute equally to one pot.

3. Our lifetime financial goals include two large sums:

   A) We bought a home. That decision alone determined a significant portion of our monthly/annual/ lifetime budget.

   B) A second agreement was to start individual retirement funds.

These factors locked in a significant share of our income, thereby making the division of the remainder much easier to determine.

4. We never check on or interfere with one another's discretionary spending.

My (our) life-time financial goals are:

1._____

2._____

3._____

4._____

PLAY FAIR

Notes from Chapter 44

P LAYING FAIR MEANS treating my partner the way I wish to be treated.

Several years ago I heard a wonderful presentation by a Federal judge. During the question and answer period following her presentation, she was asked what had prepared her best for being a judge. Without a moment's hesitation she said, "Trying to be fair while raising my children."

She said her favorite cases were patent cases. Often she believed both sides were telling the truth. She felt that both of them had done original work, and each truly believed that the other had stolen his idea. She struggled with fairness.

Over the years, as complaints have been articulated, I have heard couples complaining about being treated unfairly by their partners.

In marriage we must be as conscientious, careful, and considerate as a Federal judge when relating to our partners.

FORGIVE OFTEN

Notes from Chapter 45

S OME PEOPLE SAY, "We must forgive and forget." To that I say "no!"

A truly horrid offense cannot be forgotten. Deep emotional scars can always be retrieved. But, it is possible to give up all forms of retaliation and move on with the friendship. It may be a little tattered but at least it's intact.

Sometimes, we pretend to forgive because we have such a desperate need to be liked.

Often, the price we pay for bribing our partner into retaining a relationship is to give into their bullying and allow our boundaries to be violated again and again. Sometimes, we call this forgiveness. It isn't.

Authentic forgiveness entails not only the realization that we need to stop obsessing about the offense and to get on with our life but — an entirely new plan.

We do not serve our partner nor ourselves well when we promise and pretend that we will forget when we can't. While doing so, we may inadvertently drive that memory into the sub-territorial portions of our mind. Once there, though temporarily unnoticed, the memory will stew like a caldron filled with muck and brew. Then, when the stewing and rotting have reach their maturity, that muck is unleashed and explodes like a volcano.

By trying to forget the offense, the offended must force the memory to live in one of the closets of his sub-conscious mind. In there, the imprisoned memory acts identically to the way we act when we've been under water too long: frantically, we push off the bottom and rocket our way to the top and gasp for air.

All persons who repress their feelings, thoughts, memories, and allow their boundaries to be violated, soon develop the now famous disease, co-dependency.

In essence, the co-dependent is saying, "I didn't like what you did, but there are few consequences if you do it again." Some one who is practicing authentic forgiveness does not say, "Hit me again, harder, harder." They say, "That didn't work for me. We must do it differently in the future."

Authentic forgiveness requires us to:

1. accurately recall and report our feelings about the event to the offender;

2. agree to a new procedure in the future.

In this scenario, the offended party, in essence, says, "What you did hurt me. I'm not available for you to do that to me again. Let's agree on a new approach to try next time."

The end result of this newly negotiated way of acting toward one another produces real friends. Real friends are available, their attention is present during a conversation, they are patient listeners. They don't teach, don't problem-solve, and don't use any form of violence.

Best friends must be skilled at authentic forgiveness.

GRIEVE TOGETHER

Notes from Chapter 48

W HETHER IT IS EXPECTED OR NOT, the general criteria for *not* handling death well are:

- *Any attempt to be protected from anguish by using one or more of the coping mechanisms of denial, such as, denial of the event by refusing to face what's happening, by isolating, or running away.*

This takes many forms such as, not praying about it, not allowing ourselves to think or talk about it to ourselves, not talking about it at all with anyone ever, leaving the room when the subject comes up, excessive use of drugs — including alcohol, and caffeine to escape the pain. Refusal to read about it or watch a documentary regarding it on TV, outright refusal to either talk with, be with, phone, or write the one who is dying.

The general criteria that indicates that we are handling death well are:

- *A day by day, week by week, lowering of the wall that protects us from anguish. This gradual process is laying aside, one by one, our coping mechanisms, mechanisms such as denial, admitting that the event is real and that what is happening is unwanted and dreadful. Finally, a gradual lessening of isolating and running away slows down to a crawl.*

Good grieving takes many forms such as, praying about it, allowing oneself to think, stew, lament, rage, sulk, fret and talk about it to oneself; talking about it with selected folks; staying in the room when the subject comes up — even if one is uncomfortable and silent; a moderate use of drugs — including alcohol, tobacco, and caffeine; a willingness to read about it or watch a documentary about it on TV; a willingness to either talk with or be with the one dying. Phone calls are made, notes are written, and visits are made to the dying person.

To grieve means to feel great sorrow, to be mentally and emotionally distressed. Grieving often includes suffering, fear, lamenting, humor, anger and weeping. We need to give ourselves time and permission to learn how to grieve thoroughly. Private grieving is important, but grieving together is necessary.

Loss is a part of everyday life. Those unskilled at grieving are often so intimidated by their ugly feelings that they refuse to acknowledge them in words. The truth is that all of us acknowledge every loss in some way — some, by nervous laughter, others by moving immediately into a diversionary subject or activity; many, usually men, do so in silence. They may hope that by not talking about it, magically it will heal on its own.

Learning to grieve in our own way is one of the skills we need to learn if we are going to be mentally, emotionally, and spiritually healthy.

One of the ways we clear out and clean up our mental machinery is by crying and talking. Crying and talking are ways of reporting, first, to ourselves and second, to others, what we think or how we feel. Sometimes talking is a trial-balloon for exploring possibilities, a human way of discovering for ourselves how we feel and think about a given issue.

When a person dies and we phone or meet with the survivors, the most skilled thing we can do is get them to talk about their loss.

We can ask simply, "What happened?" or "How did it happen?" These are powerful questions that act like healing potions. Invite the survivor to tell and retell the story. It is by the telling and retelling that the wound begins to heal.

One of the most skilled things we can do to grieve thoroughly is for us to talk to ourselves about how we feel and what we think. Another powerful medicine for grieving in a healthy way is to conduct some form of funeral or memorial ceremony.

Those who have studied grieving patterns have learned that, for grieving to run its full course and to complete its task, it must be done both privately and communally. Like a pest that will not leave us alone, incomplete grieving does not go away on its own; it doesn't disappear when it is ignored. It lingers in the background until it is addressed and has had its full say.

I recommend that we establish a pattern of acknowledging every loss we encounter and that we do so soon after the loss has occurred. This means that we do not grieve ritualistically only over the death of a human or animal. It includes the loss of things as broad in scope as hopes, dreams, plans, jobs, opportunities, relationships, and health.

Good effective rituals do not need to be long and elaborate, or to include others. The ritual can be as simple as a few moments of silence or as elaborate as inviting friends to participate.

Healthy, authentic, complete grieving takes time. The grieving, healing, and recovering process is subjective in nature; it is not objective. It is so personal that we all have our own ways of doing it. Those who know how they grieve go through the experience faster than those who do not know. Some people have never experienced a significant loss and are clumsy when it comes to grieving.

A major difficulty some have with grieving publicly is the issue of vulnerability. Their self-esteem is so low that they cannot afford to appear weak or to cry. In the nearly three decades I've been a pastor, I have conducted several hundred funerals. I cannot count the number of times I've heard people tell me, "During the service I have to remain strong." This is pure garbage; only the weak, the frightened, the intimidated don't cry when there is something to cry about.

In his wonderful novel, *The Pelican Brief,* (Island Books: New York, 1992), p. 203. John Grisham describes one form of healthy grieving.

"She loved him too. And it hurt so badly. She wanted to stay in bed and cry for a week. The day after her father's funeral, a psychiatrist had explained that the soul needs a brief, very intense period of grieving, then it moves to the next phase. But it must have the pain; it must suffer without restraint before it can properly move on. She took his advice, and grieved without courage for two weeks, then got tired of it and moved to the next stage. It worked."

"Death was a subject she'd analyzed from different angles in the past ten days. Except for going quietly in one's sleep, she was undecided as to the best approach. A slow, agonizing demise from a disease was a nightmare for the victim and the loved ones, but at least there was time for preparation and farewells. A violent, unexpected death was over in a second and probably best for the deceased. But the shock was numbing for those left behind. There were so many painful questions. Did he

suffer? What was his last thought? Why did it happen? And watching the quick death of a loved one was beyond description."

"She loved him more because she watched him die, and she told herself to stop hearing the explosion, and stop smelling the smoke, and stop watching him die. If she survived three more days, she would be in a place where she could lock the door and cry and throw things until the grieving was over. She was determined to grieve, and to heal. It was the least she deserved." (p. 316-317.)

MONITOR YOURSELVES

Notes from Chapter 49

A HEALTHY BODY doesn't happen by chance. It is the result of many things, including correct eating, drinking, rest, recreation, and a managed amount of destructive stress.

Similarly, a well-built house is not the result of guess-work and happenstance. It is the result of the coming together of a myriad of factors, such as intelligent planning, knowledgeable design, and skilled construction.

Strong relationships, families, households, friendships, and partnerships don't just happen by chance, either. In their own way, they too are the result of intelligent planning, knowledgeable design, and skilled construction.

Just as we periodically take our car into the shop for servicing, and visit the doctor or dentist for a regular check up, our relationships need the same kind of care, if they are going to remain healthy. One way to assure that this happens is to keep track of the health of our relationships.

Just for fun, do the following relational check-up:

SELF MONITORING

Today's Date_____

		Yes	Sometimes	No
1.	Emulate Success	❏	❏	❏
2.	Speak Gently	❏	❏	❏
3.	Repair Yourself	❏	❏	❏
4.	Talk Respectfully	❏	❏	❏
5.	Master Conflict Control	❏	❏	❏
6.	Listen With Care	❏	❏	❏
7.	Don't Escalate	❏	❏	❏
8.	Care For That Injury	❏	❏	❏
9.	Feed Your Soul	❏	❏	❏
10.	Write That Letter	❏	❏	❏
11.	Tell The Truth	❏	❏	❏
12.	Learn About One Another	❏	❏	❏
13.	Give 10s	❏	❏	❏
14.	Reconnect	❏	❏	❏
15.	Say, "Thanks"	❏	❏	❏
16.	Give Delightful Surprises	❏	❏	❏
17.	Say, "You're Great!"	❏	❏	❏
18.	Share Your Stuff	❏	❏	❏
19.	Take Time To Be Alone	❏	❏	❏
20.	Establish Life Goals	❏	❏	❏
21.	Prepare For Death	❏	❏	❏

(continued on page 238)

(continued from page 237)

		Yes	Sometimes	No
22.	Live Fully	❏	❏	❏
23.	Enable The Needy	❏	❏	❏
24.	Establish Rules	❏	❏	❏
25.	Create Healthy Boundaries	❏	❏	❏
26.	Leave With Skill	❏	❏	❏
27.	Don't Lie	❏	❏	❏
28.	Keep Your Word	❏	❏	❏
29.	Don't Parent Your Partner	❏	❏	❏
30.	Don't Assume Mind-reading	❏	❏	❏
31.	Don't Compete	❏	❏	❏
32.	Hold Household Councils	❏	❏	❏
33.	Date 'Til You Drop	❏	❏	❏
34.	Make History Together	❏	❏	❏
35.	Establish Healthy Systems	❏	❏	❏
36.	Adjust To Your Mini-marriages	❏	❏	❏
37.	Take One Another's Temperature	❏	❏	❏
38.	Prepare For Love-making	❏	❏	❏
39.	Don't Blame	❏	❏	❏
40.	Don't Punish One Another	❏	❏	❏
41.	Don't Slam One Another	❏	❏	❏
42.	Manage Your Money	❏	❏	❏
43.	Dance Together	❏	❏	❏
44.	Play Fair	❏	❏	❏
45.	Forgive Often	❏	❏	❏
46.	Make Moments To Remember	❏	❏	❏

(continued on page 239)

(continued from page 238)

	Yes	Sometimes	No
47. Have Fun	❏	❏	❏
48. Grieve Together	❏	❏	❏
49. Monitor Yourselves	❏	❏	❏
50. Don't Be Lone Rangers	❏	❏	❏
TOTALS	___	___	___

How did you do?

❏ Very well

❏ I think I (we) could use some work

❏ I'll (we'll) do better next time

DON'T BE LONE RANGERS

Notes from Chapter 50

IF YOU WISH TO PROCEED in establishing an on-going group, here are a few suggestions.

- If you are a member of a faith-based community, civic club, recreation, interest group, or professional association, start a Relationship Discussion Group there.
- Or, start a Relationship Discussion Group made up of your friends and their friends.

Do not be stopped or distracted by thoughts and feelings that you are not up to doing this. It is easier than you think.

ARRANGING THE FIRST MEETING...

1. Simply tell several friends that you would like to meet for this purpose.

2. Tell them that the first meeting will be in your home (or some convenient place conducive to discussion).

3. Set the date.

4. Be sure to determine how long the first meeting will last.

FACILITATING THE FIRST MEETING...

1. Tell the gathering about your experience of reading this book or attending one of my seminars.

2. Use this book as your guide. Simply begin your discussion by reading from this book.

3. Allow the discussion to unfold naturally while reminding the group that "We are not here to give advice but to give support — we do this best by listening."

4. At the end of the meeting, ask if they would like to meet again. If they would, fine. If not, repeat this process until you have gathered folks who have a desire for this type of on-going networking.

The easiest way for me to become a part of this kind of group would be to: _____

_____

_____

_____

(continued on page 241)

(continued from page 240)

I will start a group myself. I will invite (singles or couples are fine):

1. _____
2. _____
3. _____
4. _____
5. _____
6. _____
7. _____
8. _____

Section 4
EPILOGUE

EPILOGUE

Having read this book to this point, you have experienced half of my message. This section brings a needed balance to this discussion. Without this, the earlier material could fall easily into the narcissistic category (self-centered and self-adoring).

There is a task even more difficult to achieve than attaining and maintaining personal psychological health, and practicing healthy relationship techniques with skill.

It is the difficult task of responding in a healthy way to portions of our society (mini-societies) that have deteriorated. Why is this so difficult? Many who are involved do not believe that they need to change. Also, the more people involved with varying backgrounds, opinions, strengths and weaknesses, and life styles the more complex the task.

Addressing collective relationship issues effectively will always be a new frontier because our minds are kaleidoscopic — they are never stagnant. Our relationships are among the first products our minds construct. This task may well be the greatest challenge of our collective life-time.

FOOD FOR THOUGHT AND QUESTIONS

1. One of the inevitable fall-outs of unhappy individuals is that they tend to have few satisfying relationships. Those they do have are often troubled and of the arms-length variety. Their unhappiness and blocks to private intimacy have public implications.

Ground-zero for starting to cure our collective ills is within ourselves. Therefore, we must all individually begin to clean up our own acts before we set out to help society at large. When we are malfunctioning, when we are plagued by continuous fear or anger, and are blaming others or society for all of our problems, it is time to look within. In almost every case, it is not possible to look within accurately without professional assistance.

What personal issue are you willing to address?

2. Adjacent to ground-zero are our household relationships. If our homes are not presently safe or healthy places in which to live and flourish, we must begin to fix them today. Whether we are giving it, receiving it, hearing or observing it, we must not tolerate battering (verbal, emotional, or physical) in our homes another minute. We must begin to repair our households and our relationships within them because that is where violence usually gets its running start. Once started, it ends up overflowing into the street, school, office, TV, congress, and into the White House.

The end-product of a safe and healthy household, where the relationship techniques are practiced with skill, is a human being who is healthier, happier, more productive and tolerant in every arena of life.

What changes are required for your household to become safer and healthier?

3. Next, in order for our nation to regain its psychological health, it is essential that our leaders clean up their acts.

The fact that leaders are constantly on TV and radio and quoted in print means that, whether they want to be or not, or even believe they are, they are our nation's most influential teachers in the acceptable use of violence.

Unknown even to themselves, many of our public leaders are lead-teachers of violence. They teach by example with their attitudes and verbal expressions, such as "war words" used against their "opponents."

War words are now the norm when it comes to seeking public office — words like "beating my opponent," "fighting," "battle," "winning," "losing." The candidates berate and are berated. If they cannot take it, they are considered "weak."

They are out of control and as "bombed" on nastiness and victory at nearly any cost, as any drunk in the gutter is on alcohol.

You who have a media presence, how does this apply to you?

4. Our nation's ills are visible, and expressed most vividly, in the sense of deep despair demonstrated and articulated by some of our youth. Their loss of hope is visible in their bodies, their language, and their attitudes.

Resignation is driving them into private conclaves, conclaves initially made bearable by drugs and distracting or numbing entertainments.

One way to begin addressing their despair is to teach every girl and boy how to be a strong, healthy wife and husband, respectively. This training should begin as early as is feasible. Your school district can hold classes which teach these principles.

How can you initiate this type of class in your school district?

5. In our rush toward accomplishment and being first, we have forgotten to discipline ourselves in the use of courtesy and proper manners. By our actions, we adults are teaching those who look to us for leadership how to be rude and insensitive to others.

Clean competition that propels us forward and toward excellence is one thing; but, when that competition includes verbal or emotional attacks, it's plain battering.

We have fallen victim to exaggerated modes of "survival of the fittest," individual freedom, and the Lone Ranger syndrome. When these exaggerations are combined with human ingenuity, they range far past their natural functions in nature. Winning, even at someone else's expense (or life), has become common place. For many, it has completely replaced cooperation and caring.

Yet, below our mad stampede to satisfy our addiction for accomplishment at any cost, we are increasingly aware that something is desperately wrong and that, if we continue much longer on this pathway, we will suffer further damage.

Is your competitiveness in balance with thoughtfulness and caring?

6. We parents and teachers must become even more vigilant in not letting our children get away with battering language and abusive behavior. Our diligence must begin by not using battering language ourselves, because we teach by what we say and do, more than by what we claim.

When we see our children battering or showing a lack of social skills, we must take time out to turn off the radio or TV, sit privately and quietly with them, and talk about how such language and/or behavior hurts, and how it is inappropriate. We must give examples to our children of how to talk with one another by the way we talk with them and our partners.

Millions of parents world-wide do this sort of thing hundreds of times during their children's lives. The long-term result is a happier human who is more sensitive toward others.

When a fighting spirit and war words are brought into a home, that home becomes a frightening boxing ring. It ceases to be a safe nest or refuge. Unfortunately, for many, their homes are the most dangerous places in their world. The home must be reclaimed as a safe place where friends help and support one another.

What can you do about this?

7. Some of the mini-societies in our world operate exactly like a dysfunctioning family. We need something akin to a Twelve Step Program for the entire nation (See Section 3, FEED YOUR SOUL, Notes from Chapter 9, page 185).

Healing our individual selves, living well, and caring only for our own, are no longer acceptable positions. Today, when one wins, we all win. When one loses, we all lose.

It is no longer possible to run away and hide from violence. The psychological and social diseases of a portion of our population are increasing in influence.

Even if it were possible to live in isolation from those most adversely affected, it would be inappropriate. We who are in the process of becoming psychologically healthy, trying to stay alert, and practicing healthy relationship techniques skillfully, can no longer build impenetrable walls around ourselves and live in comfort and isolation from others who live in want or terror.

What can you do to address the needs of those involved in destructive practices?

8. One of the saddest, and certainly one of the sickest events I've heard of, took place in Chicago. Two pre-teen boys threw a six-year-old out of an eleventh story window to his death because he refused to steal candy for them.

Unfortunately, this is but one of thousands of senseless acts of violence which are happening daily. By the time you read this page, this story will be replaced with yet another sickening "tragedy of the week."

This sort of incident has become an acceptable part of our news, our entertainment — our very lives. On stage and especially in the movies, violence has lost its "use only during emergencies" status and has been transformed into something akin to art. What was intended for fantasy only has become a life-style and first choice for many.

Explosions of hatred are so common that we have become numb to most of them. Unless we personally know those involved, we remain distanced just far enough to think that they are horrible acts but seldom feel their sickening impact.

What can you do to heal the pain that breeds such horrible acts?

9. The attention we pay to violence (and movement) is natural; we cannot root it out, nor should we. When something moves or a light flashes, we look at it without thinking or trying. These responses are a part of our God-given, much-needed defense system. In humans, these reactions combine with our great intelligence and curiosity. As a result, we have grown in vastly complicated ways. We must master our instincts, not attempt to kill them off.

We will always be attracted to violence and have a propensity to use it. What we must learn is to use it only when it is appropriate.

When is violence appropriate? My answer is, almost never!

I do not believe in universal pacifism. When rescuing a child from a life-threatening or life-long damaging situation, it is right(eous) for the parent or care-giver to be as violent as necessary against the perpetrator.

Fortunately, the vast majority of us can live our entire lives without ever resorting to violence, because we have soldiers and police to do our violence for us.

10. *Is there a place for violence?* My answer is, yes!

Voluntary violence must become a norm. As a result of collective agreements, certainly not through legislation, violence must be confined to sporting events and entertainment. Verbal, emotional, and physical violence are extremely entertaining in media, and that is wherein it must be confined. In sports and in entertainment we can get our fill as we place ourselves on a vicarious violence diet, and avoid all other types.

11. *When is domestic violence appropriate.* My answer is — never!

Violence has a ripple effect and, by nature, recycles itself. Innocent, helpless, and impressionable children first absorb, then imitate, what they see, hear, and feel. In real life, and in every form of media, what children see adults do is what adults are inadvertently asking kids to imitate.

Most adults involved in domestic violence are Survivors. Nearly all of those who practice domestic violence have been taught that fighting is acceptable, and that it is the surest strategy for surviving and getting one's way.

When two survivors who have adopted fighting as their modus operandi become a couple, often the highest skill they bring to the relationship is their ability to fight. The result? Domestic war. Domestic violence is pure street fighting — guerrilla warfare. When it happens in the home, that home has become hell.

12. Children are the only truly helpless victims of domestic violence. All others have options.

    Do you believe this is true?

13. When watching some talk shows, appropriately dubbed "trash TV," (this also applies to radio) whom are we seeing/hearing? Often, we are seeing people who are psychologically damaged. Those people should not be on TV; they should be in private therapy. By being on TV, the impression is given that they represent the norm. They don't!

Media Institutions must begin bringing balance to their presentations. I do not believe that CNN, the evening news, or newspaper headlines are an accurate depiction of the true condition of humanity, or of what's happening on our planet. To be sure, the screaming headlines do accurately portray a portion of us who are in grave danger; but, they are a minority. Often, the evening news is one great hour of deception.

A reporter, camera, or headline can focus on only one thing at a time. Their end product (which is what we see or read) reflects their nature which is microscopic, not panoramic. Our media tend to fixate on a story and magnify its importance out of proportion.

The O. J. Simpson catastrophe is but one of an abundance of perfect examples. The media's fixations on the tragic and the horrible is understandable financially. It is also understandable because of our natural propensity to stare at the unusual and horrible. However, such exaggerated coverage leads to the presumption that tragedy and ghastliness are the norm. This is the equivalent of a mapmaker's depicting the Hawaiian Islands as consuming half the globe.

I believe that the vast majority of humanity is slowly progressing and improving. However, there are segments (mini-societies) of our population that are in severe trouble and are virtually rotting. We must intervene at the central source of our rotting, and address our deterioration directly. *How?*

We can effectively address our collective dysfunctions — one individual and one family at a time.

The richest, happiest, friendliest, and most fulfilled children in this world are those who have parents who love one another.

It is possible to teach parents how to love one another with authentic personal, married, family, community, and spiritual love.

We must teach our children the skills that create healthy and thoughtfully loving relationships.

We must also teach newly emerging parents how to achieve, live, and sustain authentic personal, married, family, community, and spiritual love.

All of this is doable!

How can you instigate such a teaching program?

14. A great deal has been and continues to be written about the gulf between the Haves and the Have-Nots. This is not only an economic gap.

Some who are Haves in terms of education, opportunities, and economics are truly Have-nots when it comes to psychological health and social skills.

Where do you fit in?

15. We humans are not moronic nor are we inadequate to this task of becoming healthier in every possible way; and we are very far from doomsday.

We are a learning species. Now is the time for us to escalate "cleaning up our act." Any excuses we used formerly not to address the ills of society, have now vanished.

What are you willing to do on behalf of our greater society?

16. The prime carriers of our collective diseases are difficult to identify because, they are marbled in and, if they choose, can disguise themselves very effectively among the economic, social, educational, and vocational Haves and Have Nots.

Another part of why they are so difficult to identify is because not all of their responses to these attitudes are directed outwardly.

Often, their need to be right, find a scapegoat, or be in absolute control is directed inwardly. They may retreat and become self-destructive or passively-aggressive; i.e., folks who say they will do something but hinder any action by digging in their heels.

The signs are intolerance, inflexibility, a lack of humor and spontaneity, rigid authoritarianism, and their like. For the prime carriers, these attitudes erupt from within, like vomiting volcanoes, whenever interpreting the constitution, scripture, the evening news, or the opinions of others who dare cross their own.

The prime carriers are the extreme and humorless "type A's" of the world. Unable to laugh at themselves, they have remarkably short fuses and are guillotine-like in their judgments of others.

The shocking news is that they are not recently arrived foreigners, illegal aliens, or minorities. They are found in schools, churches and synagogues, gymnasiums, in coffee klatches, and in the board rooms of the Fortune 500. Most of us can find at least one of them lurking within our mind because —- they are us.

In what ways are you a carrier of our collective diseases? (Intolerance, humorless authoritarianism, and prejudice — to name but a few.)

17. *Who is the person or who are the people you dislike, distrust, and/or are the most prejudiced against?*

If you have already exempted yourself from this question because you "love everybody," or "are not a prejudiced person," you surely carry the disease.

Every human on earth carries prejudice; therefore, ours is a task of managing our disease rather than denying that we have it. Fear of strangers (xenophobia) — I'm writing about the broadest forms of xenophobia which include those who dress differently, listen to different music, and comb their political, religious, or philosophical hair differently —- is built into everyone of us as a protective device. To claim that we have outgrown it, or to think that we will outgrow it, is nonsense.

Today, we are not pulling together; we're pulling apart and, furthermore, we're pulling away from one another. Tolerance levels are decreasing at alarming rates. Only a few individuals of every race are able to be bi-racial with ease. The gentle-sounding, "Birds of a feather flock together," has been replaced with the frightening strategy of, "Eat or be eaten," with appalling consequences.

Race, gender, class, and cultural wars, predicted for the future by some, are already here. We are more and more dividing, living, worshipping, and studying in groups of like-kinds.

18. The causes of our difficulties are many; so must be our answers. We know that in socks, shirts, pants, and dresses, one size *does not* fit all. In healing our social and cultural diseases, we must not expect any single answer to do the entire job.

At the central core of our being, we are loving, light-hearted; and we have an incredible capacity for authentic enjoyment. We are magnificently creative. We need to turn our creativity toward healing our social/cultural diseases.

What first steps are you willing to take to help heal our social/cultural diseases?

Underlying all of the above is a problem so huge — and growing each day — that intellectually and emotionally we stagger under its weight. This problem is potentially the greatest killer of all time — over population.

Over population among the world's poorest and uneducated is great, but over population in industrial countries is even more polluting to the earth. This is so because an industrialized person produces far more pollution than does an unindustrialized person.

Some believe that the earth is capable of an always increasing number of humans and the answer is to manage ourselves and resources better. To be sure, we do need to do this, but that isn't enough.

Our planet cannot handle an infinite number of humans any more than a freeway can handle any number of vehicles — grid-lock eventually occurs. We need more than better resource and financial management, world wide. *We must reduce the number of people on earth by bringing fewer onto it.* Some of our unemployment is due to the fact that we have an over abundance of humans/workers. In America, our youngest and most willing workers are hard hit by this fact.

Currently, more than a billion people on our planet earn less than one dollar a day. Is it right to bring even more people onto our planet when their life will be a constant struggle? A struggle they will lose.

What are you willing to do on behalf of our greater society?

Are you willing to educate yourself and face the truth about the threats of over population?

❏ YES   ❏ NO

A wonderful place to begin is by reading...

Beyond The Limits, Confronting Global Collapse, Envisioning A Sustainable Future, Donella H. Meadows, Dennis L. Meadows, Jorgen Randers, Chelsea Green Publications, Mills, VT. 1992.

The Population Bomb, Paul R. Ehrlich, Ballentine, New York, 1971.

When it comes to over population, religions are major contributors. If, for any reason, your religion encourages uncontrolled growth, are you willing to pressure your leaders to change their stance?

Are you willing to purposely down-size the number of children in your "dream family" for the good of the planet?

❏ YES   ❏ NO

19. An affirmation: Whenever I find myself wanting to respond to any person or situation in an unhealthy or unskilled way, I will immediately stop myself. I will always look for non-violent ways to settle my differences with others. I will endeavor always to speak respectfully — even to those who speak disrespectfully to me. The first time I cannot control myself, I will seek help.

How can you use this affirmation? If you cannot use it, rewrite it.

20. Because social and cultural diseases are diseases of the mind and heart, the cure must begin in the mind and heart rather than at a behavioral level which, as we all know, is closer to the symptoms than to the causes. How do we begin addressing these people and planting the seeds that cure their minds? One way is by sitting with them and listening to them tell their life stories.

This suggestion may seem benign and naive; it is neither. This practice is powerful and wise. It produces great insight, eventual healing, and strength for both the teller and the listener.

Have you ever been asked, even once, to tell your life's story? If not, get the ball rolling. Ask a close friend to tell you theirs.